Zen for Druids

A Further Guide to Integration, Compassion
and Harmony with Nature

First published by Moon Books, 2016
Moon Books is an imprint of John Hunt Publishing Ltd., Laurel House, Station Approach,
Alresford, Hants, SO24 9JH, UK
office1@jhpbooks.net
www.johnhuntpublishing.com
www.moon-books.net

For distributor details and how to order please visit the 'Ordering' section on our website.

Text copyright: Joanna van der Hoeven 2015

ISBN: 978 1 78535 442 7
Library of Congress Control Number: 2016939772

A CIP catalogue record for this book is available from the British Library.

Design: Stuart Davies

Printed and bound by CPI Group (UK) Ltd, Croydon, CR0 4YY, UK

We operate a distinctive and ethical publishing philosophy in all
areas of our business, from our global network of authors to
production and worldwide distribution.

CONTENTS

Acknowledgements

A special thank you to Photography by Emily Fae once again for the wonderful cover artwork.

www.photographybyemilyfae.com

Thank you to the ancestors, especially the ancestors of tradition, whose teachings continue to inspire. May we be the awen.

Introduction

Welcome to *Zen for Druids*. This book is designed for students of either Zen or Druidry (or both) as well as anyone who is interested in following an earth-based tradition in mindfulness and with compassion. It is a further guide to my first book, *Zen Druidry*, which was an introduction through the Pagan Portals series with Moon Books. Please do read *Zen Druidry* first, as it gives the introduction, history and basics necessary to continue with this work.

In this text we will explore concepts found within Zen Buddhism and Druidry: where they meet, and where they work together to create a holistic living experience based in reverence for nature. It is our aim to live a fulfilled life, finding freedom from the constraints we often build around ourselves, and integrating our experiences in unity with mind, body and spirit.

We begin by looking at Druidry and the Dharma, examining the Three Treasures, the Four Noble Truths and the Five Noble Precepts in Zen Buddhism. We will look at the Wheel of the Year, ethics and the importance of an earth-based tradition in our modern world. We then work with the seasons in an in-depth manner that brings us into a mindful and integrated state devoted to the cycles of nature, the gods and the ancestors. We integrate the concepts of the Three Treasures, the Four Noble Truths, the Five Noble Precepts and more into our ethics and worldview. We will also study the self, the importance of meditation and of mindfulness.

What you put into this practice determines what you will get out of it. It will require daily meditation in a form that is suitable to you, as well as exercises to help you progress deeper into the heart of Zen Druidry. Keeping a journal is recommended, in order to record thoughts, emotions, set-backs and breakthroughs. Know that there isn't necessarily a goal to be achieved in this practice other than an awareness of the self, and through that awareness a life that is more integrated with the natural world. *Zen for Druids* is not about self-improvement, but rather aimed at benefitting the *whole* through the actions of the self.

At the end of each chapter there will be things to think about or questions for you to answer. There isn't necessarily a right or wrong answer to any of the questions, only the opportunity for personal knowledge to be gained through experience for future development. Remember that we are constantly learning, and using what we have gained from this text is only the beginning of the journey. It is up to you to walk it in steps filled with awareness and the blessings of life itself.

I mention the gods a couple of times, and those who are atheistic may disagree with my perception. However, a belief in the gods is not necessary to partake in this practice. You may still take on the lessons of this book without the belief in or the following of any particular deity. Indeed, in Buddhism there are no gods, only guides whose experience we may be able to learn from. Buddha was not a god. Simply skip material and questions relating to deity if you so wish; the choice is entirely yours to make.

Zen for Druids is a practical, down-to-earth approach to spirituality, philosophy and way of life. We will learn not only to go with the flow, but to be the flow itself.

Blessings on your journey.

Part One: Druidry and the Dharma

The dharma is the teaching of the Buddha, passed on for over two thousand years. It is divided into different categories, and here we will cover: the Three Treasures; the Four Noble Truths; the Five Noble Precepts; the Eightfold Path; and the 16 Bodhisattva Precepts in relation to Druidry. The dharma is offered to all, regardless of background, age, ability and so on. The Buddha transmitted the dharma to his disciples in the hope that he could help ease their suffering: the shared condition of human existence that we all experience. This suffering is known as *dukkha*. For the purposes of these lessons we will use the term suffering, so as not to confuse you with an unfamiliar language.

Suffering is experienced in many different forms. It can be feelings of discomfort, physical pain, dissatisfaction, desire, greed, restlessness, boredom and so on. So much of our lives are filled with suffering, because we are simply not in the present moment. Thankfully, there are ways to move through suffering.

Within Druidry, we see the sacredness of all things as paramount to the tradition. The wasp is just as sacred as the bee, the cat just as sacred as the leopard, the gorilla just as sacred as the human, the blade of grass just as sacred as the oak. When we recognise the sanctity of all things, our perceptions change. We become more aware of what it is that we are doing at any given moment, because we are living in the present moment. If we are living in the past or lost in the future it is difficult to act accordingly and with respect, honouring the sanctity of the natural world around us. This awareness is much like mindfulness within Buddhism (more on that later). Being awake and aware to all life around us and seeing ourselves as part of a whole helps to alleviate suffering on so many levels.

Let us take a look at the dharma and see how it corresponds to Druidry.

Chapter One

The Three Treasures

The Three Treasures (sometimes called the Three Jewels) are what all Buddhists can take refuge in, in order to alleviate suffering. They are:

- That everyone has a Buddha nature: taking refuge in the Buddha
- The dharma reflects ultimate truth: taking refuge in the dharma
- There is a community (known as sangha in Buddhism): taking refuge in the community

In today's society, we often take refuge in that which causes us harm: drugs; alcohol; high-fat foods and so on. We take refuge in violent or mind-numbing television shows. We may even take refuge in abusive relationships. All of these do not help to alleviate suffering, but only increase suffering. We need to re-evaluate what it is that we take refuge in. Let us look at the Three Treasures that Buddhists take refuge in, and see how they are reflected in modern Druidry.

Taking refuge in the Buddha: Everyone has a Buddha nature

In this teaching, we see that everyone has the essence of the Buddha within them. This means that everyone can achieve enlightenment. When we recognise the Buddha nature of a stranger, for example, our behaviour and attitude towards them will shift. We will act with more compassion, because we see that which is in ourselves, our own Buddha nature, is also within them. Within Druidry, as mentioned above, the sanctity of all nature is at the heart of its teachings. There is no hierarchy within Druidry; we are aware that we are a part of an ecosystem, part of a planet, part of the universe and part of the whole. Through the wonders of science, we know that we contain star stuff within our blood and bones. When we realise that we are made up of so many different elements, non-human elements, we are able to recognise the greater pattern that makes up life, and our part within it as a strand of the web of creation. We have rivers and oceans within us, for we drink water every day. We have the sun within us, in the food that we eat, the light upon our skin. We realise that the illusion of separation is just that: an illusion. When the boundaries of this illusory divide fall away, we can become fully integrated into the world around us. There is no human and nature, there is only nature.

There is a Zen story that states: 'If you see Buddha on the road, kill him!' This means that anything that we conceive as being external to ourselves is only an illusion, for the Buddha is within. The Buddha is our potential to live our lives in our own perfect truth, awake and aware to life all around us, fully participating in life rather than being passengers on the journey. By recognising our own Buddha nature, we see it in others. The sanctity of life and all creation directs us to live our lives accordingly.

Buddha was/is a great teacher. He exists today as he existed thousands of years ago. He is an inspiration to all who honour the Buddhist tradition. In the Buddha we are inspired to great healing, great peace. We can honour our teachers from all traditions that speak to our soul. In Druidry, we work with the ancestors: ancestors of blood, ancestors of place and ancestors of tradition. Buddha can be a great ancestor of tradition – so can the Dalai Lama, or Zen Buddhist monk and activist Thich Nhat Hanh just as much as Taliesin, Boudicca or modern-day writers and Druids such as Emma Restall Orr or Philip Carr-Gomm.

Taking refuge in the dharma: The dharma reflects ultimate truth

Truth is a tricky word in modern-day society. Yet it is central to both Buddhist and Druid teachings. In Buddhism, we drop the illusion of separateness; we step beyond suffering created by duality and merge into our own truth. Within modern Druidry, there is a saying: 'The truth against the world'. The truth is our own self, our true self, without the conditions and restrictions placed upon it by the ego and others. This self works in the world to create peace and harmony, for it is at peace and harmony. The world is that which tries to impose illusions of duality or conditions of existence upon us. We are told that we need this or that in order to be happy. We are told what to eat, wear, what car to drive. We are told that we are superior to others, human and non-human. We often believe that we will be happy in the future, as we set a condition upon our lives for our own happiness. When we drop these conditions and really pay attention to life, we find out what we really need in order to have peace and happiness. When we follow our own nature and listen to the truth within, we are able to find our place in the world. We are better able to hear our own soul's truth, and that is the truth against the world. We find wisdom in the teachings, in the dharma, and we know that through experience of the teachings we can understand the truth for ourselves. Within Zen Druidry we realise that there is no monopoly on wisdom. By combining the teachings of both Druidry and Zen Buddhism each are complemented and enhanced.

Taking refuge in the dharma, we recognise for ourselves that the real cause of suffering stems from within, as does the real cause of joy and peace. Taking refuge in the teachings of Druidry, we learn about integration with the world, and how to live our lives as a reflection of our love and devotion to the natural world around us. Both lead us to living lives fully awake and aware, lives that are filled with responsibility towards everything that exists on our planet. It guides us to live in harmony and in peace, mindful of sustainability and honour.

Taking refuge in the community: There is a community

In Buddhism, the community (known as the sangha) is there for one to take refuge in, providing support through shared ideals and goals. They are fellow Buddhists, people you meditate with, perhaps even a monastic community. They are like-minded people, on the path to enlightenment, trying to ease suffering. They are people who can help you on the path, and people that may come to you for help.

This community has been taken further in modern Buddhism to incorporate the planet, seeing and knowing that the earth is our home, our community, and therefore we must take better care of it. Within Druidry, the community is our environment. Not just the land upon which we live but our homes, our workplaces, the Druid community: everything that we are working with in the world. Druidry knows that life is all inter-connected, that we are all parts of a whole. Ecosystems function because everything knows its place in the wider context, fulfilling its role (living its truth) and thereby contributing to the benefit of the whole. We support the community and the community supports us. We can take refuge in this community, knowing on the most basic level that we are all in this together. It engenders a deep respect for the community, for the whole.

There is a Druid community throughout the world, as there is a Buddhist community. It may be difficult to find other Druids in your particular area, however, there are groups and groves, festivals and camps, Orders and organisations you can join in order to connect with other people following the Druid path, to find support in a community, or to support others within the community in a Druid context. Druidry also recognises the community as a whole, on this little rock we call planet Earth, hurtling through time and space.

Questions:

- What is it that you currently take refuge in? Does it cause further suffering? If so, what can you do to change?
- Think about the concept of everyone having a Buddha nature, or seeing the sacredness of all things. In Druidry and in Animism there is no division, no one thing being holier or more sacred than another. Everything is simply a part of an ecosystem, part of a whole. Where do you place any dividing line within your own life? Is a grain of sand less sacred than a desert? A drop of water to a lake?
- What is truth? What do you feel to be your personal truth? Stripped away of ego and conditions, what would your true self feel like?
- Look at the community of which you are a part. Is that community supportive? Do you support it? Look beyond the human realm of community, and explore the non-human community in your local environment, and in the wider world. Do you have a sense of that community?

Chapter Two

The Four Noble Truths

The Four Noble Truths really are the core of the dharma, the teachings. They are:

1. There is suffering (dukkha)
2. Suffering is caused by desire/attachment/grasping
3. Suffering can be alleviated
4. The path to the cessation of suffering can be found in the Middle Way, through the Eightfold Path

The term *suffering* can often seem a bit depressing, especially when the first noble truth simply states that there is suffering and nothing more. However, when we read on through the subsequent noble truths, we realise that even though there is suffering, we can work through it towards a path of liberation from suffering. We have a very real choice in our lives as to what to do with suffering, both our own suffering and that of others. We have a very real choice to live our lives, to really live, awake and aware.

In Druidry, we see the inter-connectedness of all things reflected in our environment, in the natural world around us. Druidry embraces the dark and the light, life and death, suffering and ease without the need for viewing them as opposing forces. Nature is neither good nor bad, nature is simply nature. Without the restrictions and boundaries placed by a dualistic view of existence, we find a deeper, better way to integrate and work in the world based on the inspiration that can be found by looking into the cycles of life all around us. Integrating this with a Zen Buddhist approach can be a real eye-opener, so let's look at each noble truth in turn and how it can be a part of a Zen Druid approach to living.

There is suffering

Just as there is great peace, joy and happiness in life there is also suffering. Humans can allow suffering to override much of the peace, joy and happiness and so the first thing to do is to come to terms with the very simple fact that there is suffering. When we open our eyes to suffering, we no longer hide from it or avoid it, we simply acknowledge the presence of suffering and in doing so, can move forwards. Suffering is a shared human condition, which can open our eyes to compassion.

A good way to begin to deal with suffering is to simply say, 'There is suffering,' as opposed to, 'I am suffering.' In doing so, we acknowledge not only our suffering but also the suffering that exists all around us. We become less self-centred, less self-obsessed and better able to work in the world for the greater benefit of all, as opposed to our own benefit. Within an ecosystem, we see how beings live and work together to create a sustainable environment that benefits the whole, in symbiosis if you will. The greater the functioning that is the whole, the better off each individual being will be. Plants photosynthesise, using energy to grow, create new forms of life, fulfilling their needs without screwing up the planet and doing it so much more efficiently than we humans have ever done. If only we could do the same! Druidry looks to nature to find inspiration, and when we see the co-operation necessary in order to survive, we understand better the simple fact that we need to be less driven by our egos and focus more of our intention on the whole. By working with suffering from a less self-centred viewpoint, we begin on our journey towards healing of the whole and a life of peace.

Suffering is caused by desire/attachment

Desire is a tricky word that has many connotations in today's society. In Zen Buddhism, desire is the wish to have things that we do not have, or to be dissatisfied with what we have and with life at this present moment. It is thinking that life would be better if we had this or that, dwelling in the past or future, desiring things (or people) to be other than what they are. Acceptance is a key word when considering the nature of desire. This is not a passive acceptance of the way things are; it is not 'giving up' because things are the way they are and there is nothing we can do to change them. We can work in the world to create the world we would like to live in, working with acceptance in the form of compassion. Compassion is working with kindness towards an understanding of the whole, widening our viewpoint beyond our sense of self and opening our hearts to achieve wholeness and peace. Attachment to desire is what causes the greatest suffering. When we suffer because things aren't the way we would like them to be and we attach to that suffering, we will never move beyond it in order to create the world we would like to live in.

Attaching to our desire causes us to be stuck in a time and place, in a mode of thinking, held within boundaries that cause us to suffer in a great variety of ways. In Druidry we move beyond the self towards integration with the whole of nature, and we can only do this when we stop attaching ourselves to our suffering. We need to see what lies beyond suffering, what lies beyond the duality of modern-day society. The blackbird does not conceive of duality, of separateness: nor does the wolf, the beetle, the sun, wind or rain. They flow on their own currents within the whole, without attachment. The tree does not mourn the falling leaf in autumn, nor does the leaf mourn the tree. The leaf falls, providing nourishment for the tree in an endless cycle of transformation and manifestation.

Suffering can be alleviated

When we let go of attachment, of desire, we can eliminate suffering. When we step beyond the ego we can work fully integrated in the world. We still require a functioning ego, a functioning sense of self that allows us to pay the bills, to protest about fracking in our area, to nurture our families, to walk the dog. Our representational ego, however, is diminished: the striving, relentless, chattering voice within our heads that is constantly dissatisfied with life, causing us to suffer, to be jealous, to be sad, to wish things were other than they are. We work with reality, as it really is, in full awareness of the present moment.

Simply acknowledging that suffering can be alleviated is a great step towards peace and happiness. Yet we attach ourselves to our suffering so much that we can even begin to take some pleasure in our suffering. This pleasure does not create happiness, but rather keeps us restricted in our own little worlds that we have created to reinforce the story of our ego, the story that confines us day in and day out because it is the path that we know. It creates drama in our lives that reinforces the self-centred ego. Most suffering is caused from within, and all attachment to suffering certainly is. Stepping off that path is difficult, and can seem daunting, yet when we do we find a great liberation. There is a Zen story that a man must want enlightenment, freedom from suffering, as much as a man whose head is held under water wants air. We must actively seek it out, for it will not happen to us. We must seek out the wilderness and wildness of our own souls by stepping off the path of suffering in order to be free from striving, from illusory boundaries that separate us from existence. We must want to be free without dwelling in or attaching to our desire to be free.

The path to the cessation of suffering can be found in the Middle Way, through the Eightfold Path

The Eightfold Path is a set of guidelines as to how to move beyond the dualities of modern thought. It sees not one way or the other, but walks the Middle Way in between all lines of thought. We do not focus on just one aspect such as the darkness or the light, but work with all aspects to fully inform our way of being. By being open in our hearts and minds, by losing the self-imposed restrictions, we can walk a path that is wholly based in the here and now, in tune with nature and its cycles.

Questions:

- What causes you to suffer? Is this suffering caused from within, or have we blamed others for our suffering? When we take a deep look at our suffering, how much can we own of it in regards to our attachment to suffering, to desires?
- How willing are you to break free from suffering?
- Are you ready to let go of your desires, of your attachments, even the desire to be free? Are you willing to be in the here and now, fully engaged in the present moment?
- Are you ready to take responsibility for your actions? Are you ready to lay aside blame? Are you ready to integrate into the natural world for the benefit of the whole, without attaching to an altruistic ideal? Are you ready to let go of the self, or at the very least explore the notion that there may not be a separate self?

We will explore the Eightfold Path a little further on, to see how walking the Middle Way can bring great peace into the world, fully integrating ourselves in the cycles of nature. However, we will first look at the Five Precepts that can form a large part of the ethical basis for both Buddhism and Druidry.

Chapter Three

The Five Precepts

The Five Precepts are the foundation for ethical behaviour in Buddhist training and practice. They contain an underlying message of non-exploitation, that is all too needed in today's world. They are guidelines to help us in making better choices in life, allowing us the freedom to choose and realising the full consequences of our choices. They are not commandments, but rather suggestions for each individual to give their attention to, really thinking deeply about each one in every aspect of their lives. When we think deeply about what it is that we do, why we do it and where we are going, then we will be able to live awake and aware of not only ourselves, but also the world at large.

The Five Precepts are:

1. Refrain from killing living beings
2. Refrain from taking that which is not given
3. Refrain from sexual misconduct
4. Refrain from false speech
5. Refrain from intoxicants that confuse the mind. (Alcohol and drugs)

In essence, the guidelines can also be viewed as a living a life filled with compassion and loving kindness at all times, being generous and also being aware of our own consumer habits, being content and at peace, speaking with mindfulness and truth and living mindfully, fully present in the moment. So, how do these relate to Druidry?

Refrain from killing living beings

What is essential to note here is the word: refrain. We know that in life we must take the lives of other beings in order to live. We eat vegetables, we cut down trees to make houses, we kill bacteria and viruses. The Druid seeks honourable relationship above all, and it is in that relationship where she is able to decide the best course of action *for her own self.* If we take for instance the issue of diet, there is a huge debate within Druidry and Paganism around what we eat, and whether a vegetarian or vegan diet is better for the environment and our own health than a meat-centred diet. The Druid will consider the issue from all angles, from the carbon emissions produced in creating a pound of animal protein compared to a pound of vegetable protein, to the pesticides and genetically modified fruits and vegetables that abound in today's world. Every possible aspect is weighed against the others in order for the Druid to come to an intelligent and reasonable conclusion that is not only in harmony with their own ethics and morals, but also in balance with the wider world. It requires thinking, research, and the letting go of ignorance in order to make a truly informed choice.

Refrain from taking that which is not given

The consumer habits of the Western world are a large threat to the environment. We are fully aware that if we continue to consume the world's resources at the current rate, and continue to enlarge the population thereby consuming even more resources, we will not be able to survive. Some even believe that this tipping point has already happened, and that humanity is now on the downward spiral of evolution into becoming extinct. What we must concern ourselves with regardless is whether or not we are taking too much. If we have established a relationship with the world around us, we will become aware of the give and take necessary for any ecosystem to function harmoniously and for the benefit of the entirety rather than its individual components. We are also reminded that generosity is beneficial to the whole, and that we should always look to give back more than we receive. We can do this by living in gratitude for what we have, and be thankful in our relatively comfortable lives on a daily basis.

Refrain from sexual misconduct

Sexual misconduct occurs when we abuse a relationship, not taking into consideration another party and acting selfishly. We are taught that intimate sexual relationships, however they may form, are a sacred expression of life itself. When the balance point tips towards the benefit of one partner to the detriment of another, then the sacredness is gone. As with all aspects of humanity, being selfish causes much destruction and anguish, so we seek to refrain from that sort of behaviour and work respectfully and compassionately with all beings.

Refrain from false speech

When we become aware of the words we speak, we are better able to create a compassionate way of life. Words have so much importance in our society, yet when we look at them closely, words are empty. It is the meaning that we place upon the words that has the power, not the words themselves. They are just words. When we hang onto a certain meaning, we can become hurt, or we can use them to hurt others. Being aware of the words we use is like being aware of holding and using a hammer; it is a tool to help us create something. We want to work skilfully with our tools, and so we are aware of the words we speak. We do not lie; we do not undermine others with our words. We use words compassionately, and where this is not possible in a given situation, then silence is perfectly acceptable. We do not gossip about others, or talk about them behind their backs. We work to create balance and harmony, to create a sustainable environment, a balanced ecosystem wherever we find ourselves.

Refrain from distilled substances that confuse the mind

Alcohol and drugs have been used for millennia in shamanic and pagan practices all over the world. However, again they are simply tools to reach altered states of consciousness, and we learn that there are other tools available to us if we desire to seek them out. Zen Buddhism is all about being fully present in the moment, aware and cognisant of all that happens to us, and our own personal actions and reactions to our external environment. Drugs and alcohol can sometimes muddy that clarity, as well as impairing our physical well-being in many cases. We must learn to be compassionate, and this begins with our own bodies. We must be aware of all that we are putting into our bodies, and whether or not it is beneficial.

The above precepts are simply good sense, when all things are considered. If we want to walk and work in tune with our environment, then we must take a deep look at the ethics we live by, changing and adapting them if necessary for a balanced ecosystem and way of life. Inspired by nature, we want the system to work beautifully and effortlessly, benefiting the whole.

Both Druidry and Zen Buddhism ask us to make sense of the teachings for our own lives, and through experience learn whether or not they are of any benefit or merit. If you disagree with any of the above, try to experience and incorporate the teaching into your life before making a judgement on it, and then if it isn't for you, don't do it. Remember, however, that Druids are working for the benefit of the whole, not just for themselves, so the actions we take affect us all, and Druidry aims to be an integral, contributing and balanced part of the whole.

Questions:

- Do you agree with the Five Precepts as mentioned above? If not, why not?

Chapter Four

The Eightfold Path and Druidry

In this section we will look at the concepts contained within the Eightfold Path and how they can relate to Druidry. Later on in further lessons we will explore the Eightfold Path in greater detail in relation to the Eightfold Wheel of the Year.

Walking the Middle Way by following the Eightfold Path we move beyond the notion of duality, of good and bad, of asceticism and indulgence, and so on. The Eightfold Path is not something that should be slavishly adhered to. The steps on the Eightfold Path are not commandments, but rather guidelines as to how to lessen suffering in your life and in the lives of others. They offer us a chance to be fully present in the moment, which allows us deep integration with the world and providing a wonderfully fulfilling relationship with all existence. Druidry is all about relationship, where soul touches soul, where the spark of awen (inspiration) is lit by experiencing the world holistically. So many people live inside their heads, and Druidry seeks to move beyond that into the wider world as part of the functioning whole.

Right View allows us to see clearly the world as it really is. We are not caught up in illusions, neither self-created nor those created by others, but simply see the world for what it is in the present moment. Like the stag, we are awake and aware to our environment, working to keep our herd together and safe. Like the river, we flow in the moment, moving around any obstacle and settling into stillness, reflecting the world around us. Druidry teaches us of the cycles of life, the times and tides that flow through nature, the impermanence of all things. Zen Buddhism also teaches of impermanence, and when we look at things with Right View we see the impermanent nature of all things, the rise and fall, the flow of the seasons. We truly see that life manifests when the conditions are correct, and dissolves when those conditions no longer exist. The energy that is life, sometimes called nwyfre in Druidry, is the only constant, for energy cannot be annihilated; it cannot be destroyed. Right View allows us to see that nature is a constant flux, that it is simply manifestation after manifestation. When we see the impermanence of all things, including our physical bodies, we begin to understand the importance of the present moment and can appreciate the beauty that exists all around us.

Right Thought (Intention) is a very important part of the Druid tradition. It requires us to focus our intention and to use that energy wisely. All thought is derived from our intention. Right Thought (sometimes called Right Intention) is a combined result of the other seven parts of the Eightfold Path that allows us to move forward knowing that our actions are honourable. We recognise the power of thought, for everything begins with a thought. When making a cup of coffee, first comes the *thought* to make the cup of coffee. We think about all the elements needed to make a cup of coffee, and then execute it accordingly. As another example, when creating a beautiful Druid ritual, we first have to think about the ritual and all that would be required. It is using inspiration, the awen to craft our intention in order to make something happen. The Druid works deeply with the awen in a cycle of inspiring and being inspired in return in order to craft their tradition and work in the world in a balanced, honourable way. Everything begins with a thought. That thought is all-important in its energy and content for walking and working in the world in order to benefit the whole.

Below is a quote from the ancient Chinese philosopher, Lao Tzu, that demonstrates the importance of Right Thought:

Watch your thoughts, for they become your words.
Watch your words, for they become your actions.
Watch your actions, for they become your habits.

Watch your habits, for they become your character.
Watch your character, for it becomes your destiny.

Right Speech is one of many outward manifestations of Right Intention and Right Thought. The importance and meaning behind words cannot be underestimated. The Druids of the Celtic Iron Age knew the importance this, remembering genealogies, histories, poems and more as part of an oral tradition. To write anything down could seriously alter the power of the words, for good or ill. It is recorded that a Druid could walk between the battle lines without fear of injury, for the Druid was the one who would tell the story later, crafting words with power and skill. What we say is just as important as what we do. Using any form of deception is dishonourable. If we are working towards the benefit of the whole, we must be honest and use our words carefully to nurture and take care of the present moment, thereby ensuring that our past will not be filled with regret and that our ancestors of the past, present and future will be proud of the work that we do. As a crafter of intention, the Druid recognises that gossip and slander are not beneficial to the whole. Speaking with the intent to deceive will not bring about peace. Speaking without forethought can cause irreparable damage.

Right Action means that our actions are what determine us, for the most part. Though thought and action are intertwined, what we *do* is highly important, for it is the manifestation of our thoughts and intentions. Within Druidry, it is not enough to read about it, contemplate or talk about it; we must *live* our Druidry. How we live our Druidry is up to us, but it should be as a part of the environmental whole, rather than a selfishly-led life filled with delusion about separation. We know that we are integral to the whole, and what we do is of utmost importance. It is about living with honour and integrity. For instance, many Druids carefully consider everything they consume in their lives, for they know that it has an impact on the whole. Many will choose a diet that causes the least possible harm, informing themselves and weighing in all the options available to them. For some, this may be vegetarianism, eating locally and organic. For others, it might be strict veganism. Yet for others, it might mean eating meat that they reared and killed themselves with the least harm, or food that they foraged and hunted in the wild. It is a personal choice for each individual, but it demonstrates how action is important in daily life. Recycling, helping in the community, working for charity, supporting others and a myriad other actions can also demonstrate the importance of action. Druidry is something to be *lived*.

Right Livelihood is engaging in work that is not contradictory to the tenets of Druidry or Zen Buddhism. It would be very difficult to be a Druid working for a fracking company, for instance, or a Buddhist owning a factory in India that produces sweatshop-made clothing. A Druid works for peace and integration in the world, perhaps by educating others on this path, in alignment with the cycles of nature and taking authority not from human-made constructs but from nature itself. In doing so, being a part of a whole is paramount, and making a living that benefits the whole simply makes sense. When we spend so much of our lives at our jobs, it should be something that is in accordance with our beliefs, or at the very least not against them in any shape or form.

Right Effort means putting the effort into living our lives fully through Right Action; we cannot have one without the other. We must be conscious of what we do and how we do it, and by being conscious we are making the effort to live honourable lives as part of the whole. We seek, with Right Effort, to abandon unwholesome states – literally those that are not part of the whole – and instead aim to nurture, support and work diligently in our practice. We know that others cannot do it for us. We must have a sense of discipline when it comes to every aspect of our lives, whether that is taking bottles to the bottle bank, doing organic gardening, working in the community, etc. Our Druidry is reflected in every single action, so we ensure that with effort all our actions will be honourable to the best of our ability. We do not fear words such as discipline or duty, for we know that we are honour-bound to live our lives with these in order to fully walk our talk.

Right Mindfulness keeps the spiritual seeker awake and aware to what is going on around them at this very moment. To be a part of an environment requires an awareness of the environment. As humans, we have misplaced our awareness with distraction and a sense of separation; however, when we return our awareness to the present moment we can act and live accordingly to the situation at hand. Neither the Druid nor the Buddhist fears reality, working firmly rooted within it. By being rooted, the connection to the spirits of place, the ancestors and the gods is stronger than ever. Being present to all things opens up a vast array of awareness that our otherwise distracted lives might have excluded, to our detriment. Being mindful is not dull; it is a re-enchantment with the world, seeing the glory and wonder occurring in the present moment, from the feel of the wind on our necks to the unfolding of a rose in the sunlight. It is driving to work in full awareness, not only of the road and our journey, but also of the cost to the planet and how we can balance it out. We are aware of all the consequences of our actions even as we are aware of the changing light as the sun sets, or hearing the bark of a dog while we sit in meditation. We bring the present moment into every aspect of our lives in order to live them with integrity. We are aware also of our thoughts, and by being aware of our thoughts, our actions and intentions are more honourable.

Right Concentration is essential to have Right Mindfulness. Our ability to concentrate on the present moment is what provides us with an awareness that is often neglected in everyday life. The Druid or Buddhist may meditate every day to improve concentration, focusing on the breath or journeying deep into the inner world to find what she needs to apply to her life in order to better achieve balance and harmony. Meditation is a great tool for expanding our ability to concentrate, and slowly trickles into all other aspects of our lives through mindfulness. The Druids of the Celtic Iron Age had to memorise hundreds and hundreds of stories, genealogies, etc. in order to recite them orally, for they were the keepers of the knowledge passed down to them. Like the Druids of old, we can be inspired by their talent and ability for concentration and work to incorporate that into our own lives not only for our own benefit, but also for that of the larger community.

Questions:

- In what other ways can aspects of the Eightfold Path be incorporated into your Druidry?
- Can you come up with your own list of how you are following the Eightfold Path? What can you change should you so wish?

Chapter Five

The Sixteen Bodhisattva Precepts

The Bodhisattva Precepts are what Zen and Buddhist practitioners can commit to in formal ceremony to show their dedication to living their life in service to the whole. In Mahayana Buddhism, the term *Bodhisattva* means, 'a person who is able to reach nirvana but delays doing so through compassion for suffering beings'. It comes from *bodhi* (enlightenment) and *sattva* (a being or essence). Being a Bodhisattva means to work in the world rather than transcend it, helping to achieve peace and compassion for all beings. These precepts and ceremony are taken very seriously. They constitute a real willingness to move beyond the self and to live a life of compassion; they are not to be taken lightly. They are a moral and ethical compass that can be a guiding force in our lives.

Within Druidry, the priest of nature is the person who lives their lives in service and in dedication to nature, to the *whole* of existence in a *holistic* sense. These precepts can be incorporated into your Druid path to help strengthen your resolve, will and determination to work in balance and harmony for the self, the community and the planet. In the San Francisco Zen Centre, these vows are taken and renewed at every full moon in ceremony: a rather Pagan way, don't you think?

The sixteen Bodhisattva Precepts are:

- Be one with the Buddha
- Be one with the dharma
- Be one with the sangha
- Refrain from evil
- Make every effort to do good
- Do good for others

- Do not kill
- Do not steal
- Do not misuse sex
- Do not speak falsely
- Refrain from intoxicants
- Do not put other people down or use slander
- Do not consider yourself above others or raise yourself at their expense
- Do not be stingy
- Do not harbour ill will
- Do not put down the Three Treasures (the Buddha, the dharma and the sangha)

The first three are also the Three Treasures, what we take refuge in. In the Bodhisattva Precepts, this is a *reminder* to take refuge in the Three Treasures; indeed, much of the dharma is inter-related or overlapping. (See the Three Treasures at the beginning of Lesson Two). We take refuge in that which will benefit the whole, instead of taking refuge in that which will cause harm. We will not go into their detail again here, but do re-read them to remind yourself of their teaching.

Refrain from evil

This is rather self-explanatory, isn't it? But what exactly is evil? From a Buddhist perspective, evil might be harming others, creating separation within the community, a multiplicity of actions that cause suffering on many levels. Within Druidry, it perhaps becomes even more difficult, for within the natural world notions of good and evil do not really exist. What we do understand, however, is that within Druidry to cause harm to the whole, to try to separate ourselves from the environment, to willingly cause destruction and, even more absurdly, take pleasure from our actions knowing that they are wrong can constitute evil behaviour. We have social and cultural codes and contracts to uphold as well, in order to function as a community. However, it is widely accepted that evil in nature is not a natural force, but rather a human construct. The hurricane that levels an entire town is not evil; it is energy following its own current, without the purposeful intention of ultimate destruction. It is a combination of the songs of wind and rain, coming together in a great force that moves and dies out dependent upon the conditions of the environment. We cannot say that the hurricane has the intention to destroy; it is merely following its own nature and the conditions set upon it by the environment. A human being, however, who kicks their dog knowing that it is wrong, or a fracking company that knows it is polluting the environment and causing cancer: this is where the difference lies. To take on the vow of a Bodhisattva we must look at every action, word and thought to ensure that we are doing our utmost not to harm others, the environment or to do anything that would be considered evil by human standards. Ignorance is not an excuse, but something that we can work on to alleviate ourselves of suffering and to refrain from evil; that means looking into consumer goods and ensuring that they are not from sweat-shop factories, for example. It is a deep investigative journey towards living a life compassionately integrated with the world.

Make every effort to do good

Ultimately, the role of the Bodhisattva is to do that: to do good. It requires a lot of effort, not because doing good is difficult, but because it requires us to look deeply into our lives to see where we need improvement towards doing good, and where we might be causing suffering both to ourselves and to others. It requires diligence. When we work with Right Effort and Right Mindfulness and when we see with Right View we are then on the road to making every effort to do good. Again, within Druidry concepts of good and evil in the context of the natural world may not be apparent in the form of a moral and ethical code of conduct; the wolf is not evil for killing the rabbit, he will not refrain from eating the rabbit in order to do good, but in a human-centred context it is of utmost importance. We must take account of the outcome of our actions on the whole environment in order follow a Druid path. Being a Druid is not just something we do, or a title that we give to ourselves. When we are a Druid we have a duty of care and service to uphold. When we are Druid we live that intention fully. Druid becomes a verb, an action. We require discipline to watch and be aware of our behaviour to ensure that it promotes harmony and union within the world. Following a Druid path is not always easy, for it requires constant work and service, as does the path of the Bodhisattva.

Do good for others

Within Buddhism and Zen, letting go of the human-centred self is what matters most, to rid ourselves of ego-centric living and to cease suffering. Zen and Buddhism come from a core of selflessness. This selflessness is not the usual modern Western interpretation of the word, though the outcome might be similar. In today's society, selflessness is seen as putting others' needs above your own. This could be to your own detriment, physically, mentally, emotionally, financially, environmentally, etc. If we sicken ourselves through altruism in order to refrain from egotism, we are not actually getting anywhere in the 'doing good' department. We have to do good for ourselves in order to do good for others. It always begins with the self, and then moves outwards like ripples in a pond, affecting the whole. Seeing the sanctity within all nature, the Druid works for the benefit of the whole as well as that which will sustain the whole. It is all about relationship: honourable and sustainable relationship. That which cannot sustain or isn't honourable is not doing any good for either ourselves or the community. We must do deep self-investigation to find out who we are, but then we must go even further rather than let the work stop there. If we allow the work to stop there, we run the risk of self-inflation, of believing the story of our self, whether told by ourselves or others, thereby increasing the chance of elevating our egos and acting in ways that defend the ego's self-importance, which for the most part are harmful to everyone involved. When we see the threads that hold us all together, we see that our strand is no more important than any other strand, and so we work to maintain the integrity of the whole.

Do not kill

This is a point of contention in many spiritual paths, for in order to live we must kill. For example, even if we follow a vegan diet we often must kill a plant in order to nourish ourselves. We take herbs and drugs to kill bacteria that might cause infection within our bodies, or to kill a virus that may spread to others. We may need to kill fleas on our pets and livestock for their well-being (and ours). Where is the dividing line between what we are allowed to kill and what we aren't? The answer to this question will differ for each person dependent upon their circumstances, upbringing, knowledge and more. Within Buddhism, most sects are vegetarian and vegan, although there are indeed some sects that eat meat. In other sects, the floor is swept before a monk walks upon it to ensure that nothing is stepped on accidentally. In this context, killing refers to other-than human animals. It is up to you to find out where the dividing line lies, where the killing line lies in your own life. What must be remembered is that it is paramount that the path you take causes the least amount of suffering in your life and in the lives around you, and that it is ethical and sustainable to the community, the environment and the welfare of all existence to the best of your abilities.

Do not steal

Taking from others without consent can cause suffering. There are some Buddhist sects where monks are not able to take anything without it being first offered (including food and drink). Most interpret this Bodhisattva Precept as stealing, rather than not taking anything that isn't offered, but both viewpoints are interesting and valid to both the Druid and the Zen Buddhist. Within Druidry, not taking more than what is sustainable is key to a good ecological environment where everything is working together. When someone starts to take more than their fair share, the rest of the system begins to fall apart. In the context of offering, it can compromise the whole if taken without consideration of the whole. Humanity has been doing this for years and it is our duty to repair the damage through living with an awareness of the whole, differentiating between our needs and our desires. Within Zen Buddhism this too is reflected in the division between the need and the desire. All of our desires may come from needs, but not all our needs come from desires. The basic needs of food, shelter, clothing and support are universal; however, they still may fluctuate widely dependent upon a person's circumstances. Someone who is unable to walk or who suffers from any physical handicap may have different needs beyond those listed above. A skilled worker may need equipment that others may not in order to sustain their livelihood (hopefully it is Right Livelihood). A starving family in a remote rural landscape may need to poach on a rich landowner's vast property in order to survive. When we take a close look at our needs versus our desires, in the Western world we see how very little we actually require in order to survive and how much extraneous energy we put into non-essentials. Taking more than your fair share can easily come under the category of stealing, especially in a Druid context. We must also honour the work of others, especially in this digital age where the concept and action of stealing has gone global: books, online courses, music, digital media and information of all kinds are constantly being downloaded illegally, without the proper recompense going to the person who created it.

Do not misuse sex

The misuse of sex causes great suffering. Within Zen Buddhism, the layperson is not asked to abstain from sex, but to not engage in harmful sexual situations (monks and nuns are prohibited from engaging in sex). Within Druidry (and much of Western Paganism) sex is a sacred act, expressing the sacred union of soul touching soul in a deep and primal way that connects us to each other, the ancestors, and the world. When this engagement of soul touching soul is dishonourable, great hurt and suffering can arise in one or all parties. Humans are emotional beings, and we learn to raft the currents of our emotions in order to live a life that is joyful and with the least amount of suffering. It is virtually impossible to separate our actions from our emotions, for our emotions are the instigators of so many of our actions. Being mindful of our emotions leads us to live more compassionately and responsibly, seeing the whole rather than our little part in the play. In a sexual context, we realise that sex without emotional responsibility isn't really honourable, though we may try to fool ourselves in that regard. What we do with our bodies has an effect on our minds, and vice versa, for they are inseparable. It is only the dualist mindset that believes it is possible, and within Zen Buddhism and all Paganism this dualist perception just doesn't work. Mind and body are connected. Mind and body are one. When we engage in harmful or irresponsible sexual conduct, we are not only harming ourselves, but harming others. We do not live isolated lives, separate from others; we are all inter-related, living together in a wonderful mash of creativity and expression, of consciousness given form. In all our interactions with others, in all our relations, we must not misuse them if we are to create peace in our lives and in the world.

Do not speak falsely

This covers a wide variety of false speaking, and not just lying or withholding truths. Often, especially in this digital age, we pass on information at the touch of a button without actually knowing the verity of the information. We can go on Facebook or Twitter to spread information at incredible speed all over the world, and this information may be false. Let us not be a part of that spread, and instead use our wits and intelligence to help us try to ensure that all that we speak, whether in person or online, is true and correct to the best of our ability. There are many hidden agendas in passing information. Speaking falsely can also cover such areas as gossip at the office or among friends; again, we may not be entirely sure of the accuracy of the information. Even if it is true, if it is detrimental to anyone do we really want to participate in increasing their suffering? What does that do for our own suffering, let alone others? The path of the Bodhisattva is to help alleviate the suffering of others, so spreading rumours, gossip and false information can seriously impede our path. We also need to be aware of exaggeration, claiming others' ideas as our own, attaching our own emotional pain to the words of others, and so on. In situations where the truth hurts, we have to seriously consider and weigh up what the outcome of our words will be, and whether it is truly worth it.

Refrain from intoxicants

What we consume each and every day really has a great impact upon our lives. This is not only what we consume physically in the form of food and drink, but also media, images, speech and so on. There are so many different kinds of toxicity around us, and it is difficult, but not impossible to be able to filter these out of our lives in order for us to help alleviate suffering. That is not to say that we turn a blind eye to suffering, but instead we choose where and when we will take it in, being utterly mindful of what we are taking in, as opposed to watching people being shot dead on the nightly news as we eat our food in front of the television. Many within Buddhism do not drink alcohol; however, many within Paganism do, especially giving offerings of mead or whiskey in the Celtic tradition. This is not to say that we should never, ever imbibe alcohol, it simply means that we show a little restraint. Refraining doesn't mean utter abstinence. Some within Druidry only drink alcohol in ritual, saving it as a very special connection to the land and the ancestors: refraining from alcohol during non-ritual times and thus making it special. The use of drugs in Buddhism is considered in the same way as alcohol; most of the time it is forbidden. Within Druidry, especially in the more shamanic practices, the use of natural drugs may help the priest or whoever is undertaking a journey to reach places that they might not otherwise be able to access within the limitations of the mind. Personally, I think that such places are available to all with enough practise and effort, and the use of drugs is simply a shortcut to that state, and therefore most of the time unnecessary. Remember Right Effort, Right Thought and Right Mindfulness? With them, we should, for the most part, be able to reach altered states without the use of intoxicants, and therefore be even more present and mindful of our experience.

Do not put other people down or use slander

There is a saying: 'Blowing out someone else's candle does not make yours burn brighter.' In our ego-centric world, especially for those brought up in capitalist societies, we are taught that it's a dog-eat-dog world; we must be top dog by whatever means possible. What we need to realise is that this is a philosophy of isolation and separation, making it easier to control single beings rather than face a multitude of beings that are working together, awake and aware to the existence of suffering. When we close down ourselves to the suffering of others, we may commit unspeakable acts in the name of self-promotion. Buddhism seeks to help everyone realise their inner Buddha nature, and the interconnectedness of all beings. Therefore, being kind to yourself and being kind to others is the only way to be in the world, sharing the enlightenment of compassion with others along the path.

Within Druidry, there is a history of a form of slander in the Iron Age Druid/Bardic tradition, where if a leader was not doing a good job, or going against the tradition or the gods/ancestors, or his behaviour less than glowing then satire would be employed. Satire brings that person back to awareness of their deeds by reflecting them back much like a mirror, pointing out what needs to be addressed in an artistic and poetic fashion. Satire was a great skill among Iron Age Druids, and it is still an art form today. However, many are unable to distinguish the line between pointing out a falsity and slandering someone, for emotional attachment to a situation causes perceptions to shift in a personal and self-centred direction, taking away the view of the whole. In short, putting others down to elevate the self is wrong, and is a tactic that shows desperation. There are a myriad ways of getting your meaning across, and standing up for what you believe in. Speaking eloquently on issues without resorting to slander or bringing others down can demonstrate true wit and intelligence.

Do not consider yourself above others or raise yourself at their expense

This works alongside the above paragraph about putting people down and the use of slander. Within Buddhism, the interconnectedness of all beings means that there is simply no way to elevate yourself above others, as everyone has a Buddha nature. It is an ego-less way of living, where instead of being driven by the ego and its self-perpetuation and self-interest we are led to a perspective where the ultimate freedom is found in the letting go of the self and in doing so, attending to the interest of the entire planet. There is no natural hierarchy. There is no hierarchy within nature, with humans at the top. Any trip out to grizzly-infested woods in Canada will confirm this, or swimming with sharks, or coming into contact with flesh-eating bacteria. The Druid knows this, and knows that we all have a part to play in the environment and ecosystem of which we are a part. The benefit to the whole of the ecosystem will also be to our own benefit. If we use and misuse others in order to elevate ourselves in any shape or form, we forget our place in the world, in the ecosystem, and create a disharmony that allows for such atrocities as war, racism, sexism, environmental destruction and any other abuse you can think of. When we forget that we are all connected, then we have the concept of 'things', and 'things' can be used and abused. In an animistic sense, there is a consciousness in all existence, and we must respect that consciousness even if we don't understand it. The tree experiences life differently from us, but we are dependent upon the tree and other plants even as they are dependent upon us, not in the least for the oxygen/carbon dioxide exchange that takes place. We have to be careful of our actions, our words, thoughts and deeds, for when we are too attached to our emotions they begin to run our lives, not allowing us to raft their currents, but instead sweeping us along in their flow. For example, we may try to undermine people in order to feel better about ourselves. When we become less interested in the self, when we see that we are a part of the whole, then the need for this sort of behaviour becomes completely unnecessary. From a Bodhisattva's point of view, and from a Druid's point of view, integration is key, not separation.

Do not be stingy

Kindness and compassion take many forms, and being generous with what we have helps us not only to feel a real part of an ecosystem or community, but also allows us to help alleviate suffering in whatever form we can. We may not be rich, but we may be able to donate some of our time to planting trees, or working at a women's shelter. We may find that at the end of the month, after we have paid our bills and other expenses, we have money left over that could be donated to a charity. We may find that a friend needs help moving, or that someone on the street is hungry. Helping others, however we can, is the true path of the

Bodhisattva. Caring and nurturing life, helping ecosystems to function to their true capacity is the Druid's gift. If we hoard our time, our money, our resources, then the rest of the system begins to break down, and others suffer greatly. Being greedy means that we are allowing others to suffer, as we are raising ourselves personally at the expense of others and consuming more than we need. This doesn't mean that we need to give everything away and go live in a monastic settlement, however; what it does mean is that we take a good, hard look at what we have, what is necessary, what we can give to others and what part we play in a world where often someone suffers because we are profiting in whatever shape or form. We have to look closely at our consumer goods, and spend our money wisely in today's society, for every penny spent is a vote for fair-trade or organic, for animal/human welfare, for the preservation of rainforest or a charitable cause in the community. It is also about showing gratitude for what we have, and acknowledging our blessings with grace.

Do not harbour ill will

Remember Lao Tzu's words about thoughts becoming words, becoming actions, etc.? When we harbour ill will against someone, we step outside the bounds of grace, forgetting what it is that we are thankful for, forgetting the interconnectedness of all beings, forgetting to raft the current of emotion rather than let it sweep us away. We have to be mindful of our thoughts in order to manifest that which benefits the whole in order to live fully integrated with the environment. When we hold grudges, we are not being mindful. We have become lost in the past hurt, and are carrying it forwards into the present moment, hurtling it towards our future and staining any prospects of peace with malice, bitterness and revenge. We fall from grace. We must, in every circumstance, open our perception to the wider world and see the suffering that exists, not just within ourselves but within others. When we are hurt, we can see that the person who has hurt us is suffering themselves. We don't have to stick around for further abuse, but we also don't hold a grudge against them and do anything such as speak falsely, undermine or raise ourselves at their expense. We acknowledge our hurt, our suffering, and we acknowledge their hurt, their suffering, and then *we let it go*. To carry the hurt with us does not benefit anyone, and only ensures the continuation of suffering.

Do not put down the Three Treasures (the Buddha, the dharma and the sangha)

This final Bodhisattva vow truly embraces the interconnectedness of all things. If we put down the Buddha, the dharma and the sangha, we are only putting down ourselves. The Buddha is within us, the possibility for enlightenment and integration. The teachings are the finger pointing at the moon; they are not the moon itself, but a guide to seeing its light and beauty. The sangha or community is the system in which we live, and we try to benefit the whole, understanding that by doing so we also benefit ourselves, for there is no separation. Do not put the Buddha down, and do not put yourself down, for you are one and the same. Do not put down the teachings, for they are simply a guide to ending suffering; the work must come from within. Do not put down the community, for you are a part of that community and reflected within it. If we see something that needs changing, we can work towards that without feelings of judgement. We learn to judge, without being judgemental. The Buddha always said not to take his words for it, rather try it for yourself first, to see if it makes sense to your soul before coming to any conclusion. This is very good advice.

Questions:

- How important is it for you to help alleviate suffering in the world around you? How connected to you is the suffering of others? How connected to you is the joy of others? How can this help you to lead a more integrated life?

- Can you spend a day with each of the Bodhisattva Precepts, and try each day to really live them in turn? How do you feel afterwards? How does this relate to the final precept?
- Look up different Bodhisattvas both historically and mythically, within the Buddhist tradition, the Druid tradition and within your own life. Can you find Bodhisattvas that inspire you in any or all three of these areas?

Part Two – The Wheel of the Year

Druidry is all about relationship with the world around us. As such, attuning to the natural world is an essential part of Druidry. Within Druidry and much of modern Western Paganism, there is the celebration of the eight festivals of the Wheel of the Year: Samhain, Winter Solstice, Imbolc, Spring Equinox, Beltane, Summer Solstice, Lughnasadh and Autumn Equinox. Some Druids do not celebrate the modern eight festivals, which were designed by Gerald Gardner and Ross Nichols in the 1950s based upon old folklore and wisdom they were able to come across. Instead, some Druids only celebrate the cross-quarter days of Samhain, Imbolc, Beltane and Lughnasadh (sometimes known as the fire festivals), and are more agriculturally based as opposed to astronomically aligned as they believe it to be more authentic to the Druid tradition of the Iron Age Celtic ancestors. We will never know for certain exactly which festival was celebrated or not by our ancient ancestors; however, the modern Wheel of the Year is a beautiful and poignant way to celebrate the turning of the seasons and the cycles of life and death. It is up to you to decide what and how you will celebrate and attune to the particular time and place of your own environment, using whatever it is that inspires you and fills you with awen (inspiration). (For more on awen, see Chapter Nineteen). For this book, we will incorporate the Eightfold Path and other elements of Zen Buddhism into the eight Pagan Druid festivals of the Wheel of the Year to find a truly unique celebratory way of living in the present moment, awake and aware to the wonders of life and living honourably within the cycle. If you are living in the Southern Hemisphere, you may want to flip the festivals over, so that they are more in tune with what is happening in nature in your own environment.

Chapter Six

Samhain

We begin with Samhain (pronounced sow-in), an ancient festival in the British Isles that marks one of two special times in the year when it is said that the veil between this world and the Otherworld lies thin. It marks the end of summer and the beginning of winter.

Extract from *Zen Druidry: Living a Natural Life with Full Awareness* by Joanna van der Hoeven:

> *Samhain, Hallowe'en, All Soul's Night: for many pagans this is the ending of one year and the beginning of another. It is often seen as the third and final harvest: the last of the apples, the cattle prepared for winter, the grain stored properly. It is also a time when it is said that the veil between the worlds is thin, and the realms of the living and the dead are laid bare to each other. We are approaching the darkest time of the year, and the killing frosts and snows await just around the corner. It is a time of letting go, of releasing into the dark half of the year, and getting rid of the dross in our lives, so that we do not have to carry them with us through the long winter nights.*

Samhain is a time to honour the ancestors, and in both Druidry and Buddhism we honour the ancestors of blood, place and tradition. Within the monastery of Zen Buddhist monk, Thich Nhat Hanh, they have developed the Five Earth Touchings, otherwise known as Touching the Earth, wherein the ancestors are honoured in the first three prostrations. These can be a wonderful way to incorporate this Buddhist teaching into our Samhain tradition, or indeed in our everyday rituals should we be so inclined. The hands are held in prayer position at the heart, and then the body is lowered to the ground so that shins, forearms (with palms facing upwards to the sky) and forehead are resting on the ground with each Earth Touching. We speak the words and then bow all the way down to the ground, really getting in touch with the earth physically and mentally, honouring it for all that it provides.

The first Earth Touching is: '*In gratitude, I bow to all generations of ancestors in my blood family.*' Here we honour our blood ties, the stories that brought us to where we are in this present moment, the history of love and suffering in our bloodlines that help to create our story today. By opening ourselves to our ancestors we acknowledge all this, and can ask for their protection, love and support. In Druidry, we honour the ancestors, and in my own tradition I finish the first Earth Touching with: 'I honour the ancestors of blood, whose stories flow through my veins.'

The second Earth Touching is: '*In gratitude, I bow to all generations of ancestors in my spiritual family.*' Here we honour the teachers who have shared their wisdom and insight throughout the years, whether we have known them personally or not. We can see ourselves in these people. These are the people who can help us to transform our suffering and bring about peace, both in our own hearts and in the world. They are the people who inspire us. In my own tradition, I finish with: 'I honour the ancestors of tradition, whose wisdom flows through the teachings.'

The third Earth Touching is: '*In gratitude, I bow to this land and all of the ancestors who made it available.*' Here we honour ancestors of place, who have made this world that we live in. They are in the soil and wind, all those who have lived and died and now exist in another form. It is the energy of the land upon which we live, that we can feel humming in our bones, if we only open ourselves to listen. In my tradition, I finish with: 'I honour the ancestors of place, whose songs flow through this land.'

The fourth Earth Touching is: '*In gratitude and compassion, I bow down and transmit my energy to those I love.*' Here we share the wisdom and insight gained from our practice and spread that out to all our loved ones in a form of a prayer. The energy we have received from the earth is given freely, and so we too give freely to those we love. We can ask our ancestors for their protection and aid in this matter. In my tradition, I end this prostration with: 'May there be peace in the hearts and minds of all those I hold dear, my family, friends and loved ones.'

The fifth Earth Touching is: '*In understanding and compassion, I bow down to reconcile myself with all those who have made me suffer.*' Here we learn that the earth gives of her energy without discrimination or prejudice, and we can learn to live magnanimously in all that we do. We understand that people who cause us to suffer do so through their own wrong perceptions, and we pray that they find a way to relieve their suffering. We work towards not holding any anger or hatred towards these people, instead trying to understand in order to better work in the world. We let go. Again, we can ask our ancestors for help in this matter. In my tradition, I finish with: 'May peace be in the hearts and minds of those who cause me and others around them to suffer, may they know loving kindness.'

Working with the ancestors can offer us a deep connection to our bloodlines, our religion or spirituality and the place that we live. It is important that all three sets of ancestors in the Druid tradition are remembered and honoured: ancestors of blood, ancestors of place and ancestors of tradition. Mystic and former Head of The Druid Network, Emma Restall Orr writes:

> *The dead fall from awareness only when they are forgotten, so the practising animist acknowledges the ancestors with gratitude and open-heartedness, each and every day – whenever a task is to be done, whenever an old tool is lifted, a skill used, an old pathway walked. When a challenge or an obstacle arises blocking the way, when pain kicks in and weakness overwhelms, it is to the ancestors that the animist turns, and it is in the ancestors that courage is found, generation to generation, hand in hand, words of wisdom*

heard and experience shared. When crises are overcome, when love is found and joy fills a moment with delight, the ancestors are an integral part of the celebration.
– Emma Restall Orr, from her essay 'Time and the Grave', from the book *This Ancient Heart.*

At Samhain it was said that the ancient Celts brought their cattle in for the winter from the high grounds, and passed them through two bonfires until their hair was singed. This may also have been performed at Beltane, at the opposite side of the Wheel of the Year. Bringing cattle close to the flames may not be entirely accurate, for it would be very difficult to get any animal that close to a fire without a major stampede in any other direction, with their instinctive aversion to fire. However, they may very well have been driven between two *smoking* bonfires, so that the smoke would cause any fleas or other little critters that came with the cattle to fall off, thereby ensuring that the cattle were both ritually and physically cleansed in preparation for their winter/summer quartering. We can use this custom at Samhain, of being between two fires when we Touch the Earth with the earlier prostrations, ending with a final purification, perhaps with mugwort or homemade lavender smudge sticks lit from the fires. Fire is a major theme for the Samhain festival, as well as at Beltane. In fact, in Edinburgh, Scotland, they hold Samhuinn (Scottish spelling) and Beltane fire festivals that are magical and wonderful to behold. Create your own fire ritual for Samhain, honour the ancestors and leave offerings for them.

Now is the time for letting go, for focusing our energy on what is important and also getting rid of dross. It means being an active participant rather than a passive observer in our lives. It is the time to collect and nurture the seeds of our intention, and to get things in order.

Samhain is the perfect time to meditate on and truly live the concept of Right Effort. With diligence and discipline we are able to scrutinise our words, thoughts and deeds to ensure that they are beneficial to ourselves and our environment. We must be disciplined, and focus intently on our practice during this very special time in the dark half of the year, for we do not want to carry forward that which will hold us back, held within bad habits, intentions or cycles. We really make an effort to walk our talk, to ensure that our actions are honourable. The ancestors are all around us, and we want to do right by them, and do to right for future ancestors to come.

Some things to consider during the Samhain tide, from Samhain to the Winter Solstice are:

- Meditate each and every day, with a combination of zazen or mindful sitting (see Part Three of this book) and ending with prayers to the ancestors (or vice versa).
- Think before you speak. Say little, think deeply.
- Sit in quiet darkness for some time each day, reflect on the nature of darkness, the dark half of the year.
- Sit quietly with your thoughts on death and dying. Contemplate the notion that energy cannot be annihilated, that everything is impermanent and that all matter is consciousness given manifestation for however long or short a time. Everything is in a state of constant change and flux, manifesting when the right conditions are met.
- Keep an altar to the ancestors, with photographs, memorabilia, etc. Spend time with your altar every day.
- Contemplate your own death; really come to terms with your own mortality (in the sense of the manifestation of you in this body) and your immortality (the fact that energy cannot be destroyed).
- Ensure that you have a Will that is up to date, and funeral plans so that when you die your loved ones will know your wishes. Write down a list of all financial investments, bills, etc. so that should a loved one have to arrange things, they

will be able to do so with as much ease as possible during a very difficult time.

- Take stock of everything that you own in the material sense. What would happen if you died tomorrow? Would there be an inordinate amount of 'stuff' for your loved ones to deal with? What can you do right now to rid yourself of all that you do not need? Go through cupboards and wardrobes, clearing them out of everything that you do not use and donating items to charity. Think deeply about living more lightly on the planet, simplifying as much as you possibly can.

- Go outside into the night, if you are able and it is safe. Learn about your environment after the sun goes down. Explore the paths and hedgerows. Learn about the night sky.

- Look deeply into your thought patterns, habits, speech, actions and behaviour. Do not ignore the darker aspects of yourself, or those parts of you that are difficult to acknowledge. Sit with any difficult feelings and emotions, and hold them with loving kindness until they ease. Then let them go.

- Meditate on what Right Effort means, and then live the concept fully.

- Review the year, and separate the wheat from the chaff. Look at what has been successful, and what has not. Take forward the seeds that you wish to plant next year and keep them safe. Let them rest a while in the darkness.

Chapter Seven

Winter Solstice

We now move on to the Winter Solstice, the shortest day of the year, which occurs around 21st-23rd December. It marks the time when the days begin to lengthen from the longest darkness, and the shift from darkness to light happens every day until the Summer Solstice.

Extract from *Zen Druidry: Living a Natural Life with Full Awareness* by Joanna van der Hoeven:

> *This is the time of the shortest day and the longest night, and the shift out of the deepest darkness towards lengthening days with more sunlight occurs. In Britain, where the days can be terribly short, especially on dark, overcast wintry days, this shift towards the light half of the year is very remarkable and special for some people, not least those who suffer from Seasonal Affective Disorder. It is a time of darkness, of quiet contemplation and of family. Bringing sprigs of greenery into the home to decorate the hearth and integrate the natural world with the inner sanctums, and the giving of gifts that is now traditional at this time of year, strengthens the family and community bonds. It is a time for rest, as the earth lies dormant, seeds waiting below ground for the return of the sun even as the cold winds blow.*

If we pay attention, we are able to see that the sun stands still on the horizon upon rising and setting during the three days around the Winter Solstice (and the Summer Solstice). Solstice means 'standing still', and we can observe this phenomenon until we begin to see the sun rising again further towards the east and setting further towards the west after the Winter Solstice. Here in Britain, we know that our pre-historic ancestors considered this a very special time as there are many ritual places aligned to the Winter and Summer Solstices. We can reflect on similar importance in our own lives as we attune to the cycles of nature.

In the British Isles, the season of darkness is very apparent in its northern latitude. Even though we have electricity, we cannot deny the effect that the darkness has upon our psyche, upon our bodies and upon our behaviour. We may attempt to drive away the darkness under the auspices of seasonal and holiday joy in the form of Christmas lights, lighting up our streets from the beginning of November onwards. However, as Druids we acknowledge the power that darkness holds, and work with it instead of trying to ignore or hide it. We know that seeds require a period of time in darkness below the ground before they begin to germinate. The human being begins in the darkness of the womb. In temples and places like Newgrange, the darkness is honoured as well as the returning light, providing that bright spark that allows the seed to break free and fulfil its potential. In the tide running up to the solstice, we honour the darkness and use that time for meditation, for reflection and for personal development. It is a time of quiet peace, where in nature we see the world around us settling into stillness. Many birds have left, the insects are hibernating or have died off, the leaves are down from the trees. The air is quieter, less filled with noise. So too are our hearts, if we follow the natural rhythms we see in our own environment.

When the solstice occurs, we have already spent our time in darkness with Right Effort, and now the tide turns towards Right Mindfulness. We begin a new cycle into the light half of the year, and so from this moment onwards we focus on bringing attention to every aspect of our lives. In doing so, we will set ourselves up rightly for what is to come.

Right Mindfulness is paying attention to our thoughts, our actions, our behaviour, our patterns and our environment. It is becoming aware of each moment, of truly understanding that life is to be lived, that it is not a passive ride to be experienced. Life is not entertainment, though it can be greatly enjoyable. Understanding the true nature of reality, of the present moment, without bringing in excess baggage from our past or worries about our future allows us to really live in the moment. It also allows us to find a great peace, where the chattering of our self is left behind in the wonder of the present moment, with its myriad songs that abound.

This time of year provides us with the chance to really study and reflect on our behaviour. Here in the Western world, it is known to be a season where peace and goodwill are desired. We can only achieve peace and goodwill if we are at peace with ourselves. We can only wish good for others when we are able to see good in ourselves. In order to do this, the lessons that we have learned from Right Effort will help us on the path to Right Mindfulness. We know the value of discipline, and we can apply that to our self-study.

With meditation, we can look deeply into our sense of self, into our being so that we can come to understand our own patterns. Understanding why we behave the way we do, why we react to certain situations, why we have developed certain habits can help us to find a greater freedom and pave the way to a path of peace. It requires courage to be able to face aspects of the self that are less than pleasing. We look within to see that we are striving, that we are vengeful, that we are angry, that we are hurt, that we are bullies, that we consume too much and so on. As the growing light of the season shines upon our souls, we can begin to see that which needs addressing. We can become more active instead of reactive when we are more self-aware. Most (but certainly not all) of the drama that we experience in the comfortable Western world is self-created and we have to learn that the world is more than just our sense of self. We have to pay great attention to our self, to see what is holding us back from hearing the songs of others. Equally, we have to let go of that sense of self, in order to truly live in freedom. Understanding our sense of self, we let it go, so that we become part of the wider web of existence, a real functioning part of the environment.

Mindfulness is simply the art of paying attention. In Zen Buddhism, it is centred on zazen: sitting meditation. When we are able to sit in mindfulness for a length of time, without getting wrapped up in our sense of self, we are able to bring that into every aspect of our lives. Mindfulness isn't just for when we are sitting and meditating, but also when we brush our teeth, walk the dogs, wash the car, read a book or listen to a friend. We stop the chattering self and really pay attention to what is going on, what someone is saying, what we are feeling through our fingertips, the sounds and scents around us. We are helped with the strength of Right Effort.

When we are mindful, we are able to see that the universe exists in everything around us, and that we are not separate. We see clouds in our glass of water, because we are mindful. We see our parents in the shape of our hands, because we are mindful. We see the sunlight in the leaf of a tree, because we are paying attention. By stopping the self-centred attention that we have lived with perhaps all our lives, we turn our focus outwards so that we don't miss a thing. We learn the joy and peace that comes from really living in a mindful manner.

Some things to consider from the Winter Solstice to Imbolc tide are:

- Meditate each and every day, for at least twenty minutes if possible. (See Part Three of this book for more details on the practice of meditation).
- If you have not done mindfulness meditation before, try the guided Mindfulness Meditation included in this book (see Chapter Fifteen). Use it as often as you must, and then work alone in your meditation when you feel ready.
- Take one day out of your week, if possible, to make it a

Mindful Day. Spend the day without television or radio, without telephone or text, without media of any sort. You don't have to sit on a cushion meditating every minute, but stop the external chatter first and foremost. Then, use your day to meditate with mindfulness. You can also clean your home in mindfulness, pet the cat, do some gardening. Do some quiet things in full mindfulness. If you can't manage an entire day, try doing a mindful hour each day. Do not get lost in thought. Do not be distracted. Be present. Be right here, right now.

- Dream. Think about the goals and intentions for the coming year. Visualise them as seeds that you have collected from your past experience, holding onto them from the last harvest at Samhain. What can you draw from the powers of darkness to nurture these seeds through until spring? Now it is time to think of their potential.

Chapter Eight

Imbolc

The days are becoming longer, and though the air is still cold, the first signs of spring emerge.

Extract from *Zen Druidry: Living a Natural Life with Full Awareness* by Joanna van der Hoeven:

At Imbolc we welcome the lengthening days and the first of the flowers, with the snowdrops coming into season. For those that celebrate by the calendar, Imbolc occurs on the 1st February, though some celebrate on 2nd February. Imbolc is the time when the sheep begin to produce milk: ewe's milk, which is where we get the name Imbolc from. For our ancestors, this was a celebratory time, when cheeses and butter could once again be made to replenish the winter stores. The milking time can occur anytime in February onwards; it's always a joy to watch the fields and wait to see the new lambs scampering, flipping their ridiculous tails! This is a time for preparing the seeds of what we wish to achieve in the coming year, dreamt up over the long winter nights, but not yet ready to plant. We must still keep these dreams safe. With Zen, we can apply Right Concentration to this time of year, and focus on total immersion in the present moment.

As we have been using Right Mindfulness in the time from the Winter Solstice to the time of Imbolc, we will notice in our environment when the first snowdrops come out, the increasing amount of sunlight each day and the slow warming of the earth. We will feel the energy softly changing, moving from an introspective feel outwards towards the growing light.

The festival of Imbolc is one of gentle joy. Agriculturally our ancestors in the British Isles celebrated the time of lactation, when ewes first began to produce milk. The winter stores could be replenished with fresh milk and cheeses, to last the hungry time through spring until the land began to offer her bounty once more and awake from her winter's slumber. Imbolc is also a Fire Festival in the Celtic year, along with Samhain, Beltane and Lughnasadh. The goddess Brighid has long been associated with this festival. She is a goddess of fire and water, of healing, poetry, smithcraft and more. This festival became Christianised as Candlemas, again showing the fire aspect of this time. The growing sunlight is reflected through earthly fire and flame. There are many ways to celebrate Imbolc, including household blessings, the making of Bride dolls and Brigid's crosses.

Become aware of how fire is a central aspect of your life, in all its manifestations. Give thanks when your central heating comes on. Give thanks for the sunlight that keeps our planet from becoming an ice cube hurtling through space. Give thanks for the gas that powers your stove/cooker, allowing you to have a hot meal. Look into a candle's flame, or a fire in the hearth, and commune with the spirit of fire. Look at how fire is manifested within the body, in energy, emotion and more.

The Druid pays attention to her surroundings. With Right Concentration (sometimes referred to as Right Focus) she can hone her skills in mindfulness. Concentrating on being fully present, little will escape our attention and we will live a more integrated life with the natural world around us. Right Concentration is a skill that can be achieved through daily meditation (see Part Three of this book). We begin with focusing on the breath and the body in meditation, and keeping our concentration centred within. We then move that focus outwards, without losing the concentration that keep us from distractions, from our chattering 'monkey mind'.

It is easy to berate ourselves for not having enough concentration in our lives. In fact, when we look at modern-day society, we see that we are being bombarded by things that actually lessen our ability to concentrate for any period of time. We have smart phones that allow us to stop whatever it is we are doing at any given moment (apart from driving, we hope!) and look at or think about something else, thereby distracting us from our original intention. We have telephones that ring us when we are at home. We have television programmes, sometimes divided into 4-7 minute segments (mostly in American shows) with advertising breaks in between. Our attention spans are becoming shorter and shorter simply through the media that we use. Twitter has a 140 character length, and if you can't communicate what you have to say in that short space then you can't say it at all. The Vine app makes looping videos that are only 6.5 seconds long. The list continues.

We have to relearn how to concentrate, how to bring our awareness in directed focus on a subject in order for our minds, bodies and lives to begin to settle once more. As infants, we absorbed information in rapt attention, no matter if it was a light shining overhead or our mother's voice. Toddlers exploring the world are intensely focused, beginning with their first steps and then on their goal. We begin to lose our abilities to concentrate with all the information we have to hand, thinking that we can absorb it all without actually realising the repercussions it has on our lives. Technology has advanced so much that our human bodies simply aren't able to cope with the information overload, and we need to take a step back and refocus.

Most of the information we are receiving is not necessary to our daily functions. Reading some celebrity's tweet will not put dinner on the table. Checking replies to our Facebook status will not get our toilets cleaned. If you've spent a media-free day a week during the Winter Solstice to Imbolc period, then you probably have realised the benefit of stopping the information overload.

We begin with a simple candle meditation, incorporating the fire aspect of the season and the one-pointed focus required in this meditation. Sit before a candle, and simply watch its flame. When thoughts arise, notice them by saying, for example 'lunch' or 'meeting' or 'cat' and then let each thought go, returning your focus to the candle's flame. If you have a family, it might be better to do this meditation either early in the morning or late at night when everyone is in bed. It doesn't matter how many times you have to bring your focus back to the candle, what matters most is that you do it. Bring your attention and concentration back however many times you need to. Concentration is a skill, and any skill is something that is developed over time. It doesn't happen in an instant.

Now is the time to take it a step further. Literally.

Walking meditation is a brilliant way draw focus into what we are doing, and help us to integrate with our natural surroundings on the Druid path. We can think of each step we take as kissing the earth, celebrating our love for life on this planet. Walking meditation (kinhin) began as an interlude to zazen, or sitting meditation, to allow the meditator to continue with their meditation while easing their body from a sedentary pose to a moving one, allowing for good circulation and bringing some exercise into the practice.

Walking meditation can be done indoors or outdoors. Zendos (Zen centres) will accommodate both practices in their buildings, but incorporating the Druid path into our spirituality means that we need to engage further with the natural world around us. Remaining indoors has its benefits, enabling us to concentrate better with fewer distractions, however, we can practise this outdoors with great joy. We can then let this practice become part of our lives to such an extent that we walk mindfully, aware of our movements wherever we go, whatever we are doing. It requires Right Concentration. Do what you can, whether indoors or out.

Not only will we benefit personally from walking meditation, but the land will benefit as well. If we walk with love and with joy, instead of walking with anger or suffering, the land will also share in this experience. Too often we believe that we are the only beings able to experience, however, we can walk in the rain and experience the rain, knowing that the rain is also experiencing us. Let us make this a good experience.

With the exercise and fresh air, we also release stress and anxiety, as we are developing a practice that allows us to be in the world by silencing our monkey mind and embracing the world as it really is.

If you are lucky enough to have a back garden this is an ideal place to begin. It is out of doors, and relatively quiet, safe and secure. If you don't have a back garden, you can try a local park that you feel is safe and secure, or a botanical garden, or even a friend's back garden (with their permission, of course!). If you live deep in the heart of a city and don't feel that you are able to access public parks with safety on your own, ask a friend or relative to join you. If you have wild stretches of forest or heathland at your doorstep, go for it, but do ensure that someone is aware of where you are going, and what you are doing. Again, take someone along if it makes you feel more at ease. If you have a young family, doing walking meditation with them is a great way to spend time together.

Barefoot walking is a great way to bring focus and attention to each and every step. However, it depends on your circumstances and whether this is a safe thing to do. Broken glass and other debris on city streets are not conducive to good barefoot walking meditation; neither is walking through gorse-laden brush in adder country. Be safe and responsible.

Really notice the feel of movement in your body as you slowly take one step, then another. Engage your whole foot in the step, touching the ground with the heel first, then rolling all the way to the tips of the toes. Be aware of what both feet are doing at the same time. This is surprisingly difficult at first, but it will hone your concentration. Breathe mindfully as if in meditation. Feel the air on your skin, the sunlight or the rain. Notice the light or darkness, the sounds and scents. Do not become lost in these, however; simply notice. Notice without judgement. You can even say to yourself 'sunlight', 'dog barking', 'snowdrop', 'icy path' and allow your awareness of everything to keep you going. When you find the mind starting to wander, or you feel you begin to judge something, bring your attention back into your feet and your breath.

Walk as slowly or as quickly as feels comfortable. Most Zen walking meditation is done slowly, but some Zen centres do practice *kinhin* quickly, to get the blood flowing and as a form of exercise. As with everything, mindfulness is key. Do this every day if you can, noticing how your environment is changing through the seasons.

Some things to consider from Imbolc to the Spring Equinox are:

- Look at how fire manifests in your life. Look at the inner fire within. See how fire can destroy as well as bring nourishment and comfort. Learn how to harness the power of fire responsibly.
- Do the candle meditation each day, and then begin walking meditation after you have sufficiently honed your concentration with the candle meditation.
- Be kind and gentle with yourself. This is a season that can be difficult, even as it was for our ancestors, who lived through the lean months of spring until food sources became more abundant.
- Do a house-blessing – research various forms or come up with your own.
- Prepare the seeds of your intention that you kept safe over Samhain and dreamt over during the Winter Solstice. Find out what will be required to bring them into fruition, but do not plant them just yet. Wait until the sun is a little

stronger, the air a little warmer, and life generally a little more forgiving. Learn the value of patience.

Chapter Nine

Spring Equinox

Day and night are of equal length, and the balance will tip over into longer days, leading us ever towards summer.

Extract from *Zen Druidry: Living a Natural Life with Full Awareness* by Joanna van der Hoeven:

The Spring Equinox is one of two very special times of balance and of change. It is a liminal time, a time that hovers between two realities, waiting to see what will befall. The tides are changing over, and at this time the day prevails over the night, when the days become longer than the nights, the sun rising and setting further apart along the horizon. It is a time of change: we can stand on the precipice, waiting to see what happens, until we lose our balance, are pushed or jump headlong into our lives. The greening is just about to happen; nature is about to explode in riotous growth, blossoms beginning to appear. It is also the hungry time of year for our ancestors, when the winter stores were running very thin, but the crops in the fields were not yet read. Food was scarce, and spring claimed more deaths than winter ever could for those who lived off the land.

When we think of spring, we think of apple and cherry blossom, of seeing more green appear in the landscape, of buds, flowers and bees. Yet for our ancestors, spring was a very difficult time, a very lean time when the winter stores were nearly depleted. If the winter was long, then there would have been a hungry time, especially if the cold and frost kept spring at bay. Yet our ancestors were also extremely resourceful, and much of their knowledge can be regained if we bother to look hard. There are many early edible plants available at this time of year, such as the first nettles. Wild food such as nettles would have been a large part of our ancestors' diet, providing much needed vitamins and minerals when there was little else to be had. If at all possible, take a wild food foraging course during the spring, summer and autumn, to allow you to be able to identify and safely eat what is growing in your local area. This can bring you more in tune with your environment and the ancestors.

This is also the time of year when we feel the impetus towards summer, the beginning of the expectations and anticipation that summer will bring. Many farmers will be ploughing their fields at this time, after harvesting the last of the winter vegetables. There is a lot of activity going on in the countryside, including migratory birds, deer beginning to break off from their large winter herds to give birth, and more. Many people feel an upsurge of energy at this time of year, and use that energy for things such as 'spring cleaning' the house. Our energy turns away from inward self-reflection and focuses more externally to the environment.

Spring cleaning is a wonderful way to get the ball rolling when it comes to clearing out energy and making space for the new vital force we feel flowing through the land at this time of year. At Imbolc, we may have blessed our home, and now we use the motivating energy of the sun for the more mundane purpose of physical, as opposed to spiritual cleansing. Really give your home a thorough clean, using natural products if you can, and see if you feel any different afterwards. Dust the blinds and mop the floors, get into all those nooks and crannies. This is also a good time of year to sort out your wardrobe, perhaps putting into storage the heavy winter coats and jumpers and getting out the lighter clothing. Anything that you haven't worn for over a year can be donated to charity. Take a deep look at all your belongings now, if you didn't do this at Samhain. Do you love them? Do you need them? Or is some of it just clutter? If so, take all the clutter, put it into a box and hide it away, perhaps in the loft, garage or a closet. If you haven't missed seeing or having these items by the Autumn Equinox, chances are you probably aren't attached to them and can give them to charity, or have a garage/car boot sale. Simplifying is always a good thing to do.

Spring is a great time to focus on Right Intention. We have worked with Right Concentration, and so we use that focus to help us choose wisely. We are planting the seeds for the rest of the year, and we want those seeds to be good seeds that will give us much nourishment. Zen monk Thich Nhat Hanh speaks of the seeds we carry within us, such as the seed of anger, the seed of compassion, the seed of laziness and the seed of joy. We have both positive and negative seeds within us all the time. The importance isn't necessarily on the positive and negative seeds within us, but rather which seeds we will tend to and water. When we water the seed of anger, we become angry. When we water the seed of compassion, we become compassionate. We don't have to water the seeds that will cause us or others to suffer. Instead with Right Intention we work to bring harmony and balance, joy and peace at the returning light in our lives.

Your mind is like a piece of land planted with many different kinds of seeds: seeds of joy, peace, mindfulness, understanding, and love; seeds of craving, anger, fear, hate, and forgetfulness. These wholesome and unwholesome seeds are always there, sleeping in the soil of your mind. The quality of your life depends on the seeds you water. If you plant tomato seeds in your gardens, tomatoes will grow. Just so, if you water a seed of peace in your mind, peace will grow. When the seeds of happiness in you are watered, you will become happy. When the seed of anger in you is watered, you will become angry. The seeds that are watered frequently are those that will grow strong.
– Thich Nhat Hanh in Anh-Huong & Hanh, Walking Meditation, 2006

What sort of seeds do you intend to plant? Think deeply about the seeds that you water and plant each and every day. Know that you will reap what you sow. With great care, we can now plant the seeds that we have kept over the winter, planting them with Right Intention, and keeping a watchful and mindful eye on them so that they will not fail should anything unforeseen happen. We take the hard work we have done over the winter by looking inwards, and now begin to extend that outwards. We walk forward into the lengthening days in mindfulness, inspired by the growing light. We get outside more and more as the weather turns more favourable. We watch the sun rise and/or set each day, and feel where we are within the cycle of our own environment.

This is also a great time to consider and begin to develop your own garden. If outdoor space is an issue, you can begin with a small window box and perhaps grow some herbs for cooking. Take the time to learn how to grow something from a seed into fruition. Learn how to do things organically. Read up on permaculture. Allow what you do in your garden to reflect the inner workings of your mind. Keep it well-tended, for if you are lax, too many weeds will soon spring up. Mindfulness in your garden and within your own mind are essential to keep things in balance.

Plum Village Monastery offers what is known as the Pebble meditation. This is an excellent meditation for this time of year, when thoughts of freshness and clarity, freedom and solidity are in our thoughts. Try this meditation daily, to help you focus on Right Intention at this time of year.

Sit up straight and relaxed and place four pebbles on the ground next to where you are sitting. Breathe in and out three times with mindfulness. Then pick up the first pebble and say:

'Breathing in, I see myself as a flower. Breathing out, I feel fresh. Flower, fresh.' (3 breaths)

The keywords we continue to practice silently are 'flower, fresh' and we breathe together quietly for three in and out breaths, really being a flower and becoming fresh. The next three pebbles are:

'Breathing in I see myself as a mountain, breathing out, I feel solid. Mountain, solid.' (3 breaths)

'Breathing in I see myself as still, clear water, breathing out, I reflect things as they really are. Clear water, reflecting.' (3 breaths)

'Breathing in I see myself as space, breathing out, I feel free. Space, free.' (3 breaths)

End with three deep mindful breaths.

Some things to consider while working from Spring Equinox to Beltane are:

- Take some wild food foraging courses in your local area.
- Do the house cleaning and clear-out suggested above.
- Watch the sun rise/set each day, noting its movement along the horizon with each passing day.
- Listen for the birds as they begin to sing more. The silence of winter slips away into the songs of spring.
- Look at the traditions of this time of year, such as Easter egg painting. Research the meaning behind some of the folk customs and see if you can incorporate them into your journey if they hold something special for you personally.
- Look up the actual date of the equinox. If you are able, try to hold a ritual at this exact time. Do you feel the tipping point towards summer, longer days and shorter nights? How does that make you feel?
- Try the pebble meditation every day, or at least once a week.
- Grow something, anything, in a garden. Bring to it your attention, focus and concentration. Be diligent, and do not allow any weeds to grow. Water and nourish it appropriately. See this reflected in your state of mind.
- Look deeply into your intentions, and choose what you

will water this year. Know that the seeds you choose will be those you derive nourishment from, so make them positive, healthy seeds.

- Give yourself a day, if you can, to look deeply at the seeds of your intention, and write them down so that you will not forget them. You will be returning to these seeds throughout the summer and autumn. Sow the seeds of deep transformational change both within and without.

Chapter Ten

Beltane

The natural world has come alive at this time of year, the May (hawthorn) blossom is out, birds are mating and the earth is warm to the touch. It's Beltane, another Celtic fire festival!

Extract from *Zen Druidry: Living a Natural Life with Full Awareness* by Joanna van der Hoeven:

At Beltane, or May Day, on the 1st May all life rejoices infertility. The hawthorn, or May bush, is usually in bloom at this time of year, and in nature we see the beautiful mating game, the dance and the courtship that will hopefully produce something wonderful later in the year. The sap is rising in the trees and in our own blood, and we feel rejuvenated, alive in the beauteous glory that the coming summer will bring. It is a time of expression, a reminder of the cycle in that every inhale must have an exhale, and so we release into the tides of summer, riding the waves of energy that pulsate through the land. At this time of year we are all young, no matter what our years and it is important to have the Right View. Living in the moment we see that life is impermanent, though we may feel immortal at this time of year. With the knowledge of the impermanence of life, of its continual change, we come to an understanding that everyone suffers, and we begin to attain the wisdom to see the nature of all things.

Who in UK countryside has not heard about or seen a Maypole Dance, or the Morris Dancers welcoming in the summer? Many village pubs throughout the countryside will have some form of celebration at this time of year, which is a designated bank holiday weekend for the first weekend in May. Beltane celebrates the first day of summer for our Celtic ancestors, at the opposite end of the Wheel of the Year to Samhain, which heralds the beginning of winter. Cattle would once again be driven between two fires before leaving for their summer pastures, and indeed fire is still a large part of this festival today, with many different ways to celebrate.

As Druids, we celebrate the rising sap of the trees, the energy of the land moving, growing upwards towards the sun that will be at its height in around seven to eight weeks' time, at the Summer Solstice. But for now, we laugh and smile at the warmer days, the longer evenings, the bright blossom and the songs of the birds. We are inspired by that energy, to bring into the physical what has perhaps remained only in the spiritual. At Beltane, we make things happen.

This is often considered a time of great fertility, though as we know mating and courtship occur all the year round in the natural world. Red deer and fallow deer rut in the autumn, for instance, while the muntjac deer prefer the heady blossom-scented heat of a July night. We see the greening, however, all around us, as plants come into their own, the perennials reaching for the sun in a cycle repeated year after year. Jack-in-the-Green is wide awake, and this is the time of growth, before the choking period of August when the riotous growth begins to battle for dominance. The Victorian Maypole Dance can be regarded as a phallic symbol of potent sexual energy, disguised for the genteel nature of that time. Morris Dancers with bells and sticks wake up the earth with their dancing, often climbing onto sacred hills to perform on May Day to greet the rising sun.

Look around you and see what has come fully awake. Attune to that energy, for it is rising, always rising until the solstice just around the corner. My personal experience with the energy of the land comes in the form of a great white serpent, that rests below the earth from Samhain to Imbolc, where it begins to rouse and rise towards the growing light. I've seen and felt this serpent energy in meditation, sitting or lying upon the land, opening my soul to the experience many times and at different points in the year. At Beltane, this serpent energy explodes high into the air. We can welcome this energy into our lives, but it is not for the faint-hearted. It is akin to the kundalini energy of yoga and tantric systems, but differs in that it lives outside of the body and in the land itself. However, when we come into contact with the serpent of the land, we may indeed awaken the serpent within. Energy does not necessarily remain within set boundaries.

We begin to understand ideas of impermanence, even as the snake sheds its skin. Nothing can remain constant, everything is in flow. All manifestation is in a process of continual transformation, from the acorn to the oak and back to the acorn again. When we begin to see these mysteries being presented to us in nature, and welcome their existence in our lives, we deepen our perception both internally and externally. We begin to develop Right View, seeing with the eyes of compassion. We begin to understand the nature of reality.

Right View is developed by understanding the Four Noble Truths: that there is suffering (dukkha); suffering is caused by desire/attachment/grasping; suffering can be alleviated and that the path to the cessation of suffering can be found in the Middle Way through the Eightfold Path. Essentially, Right View helps us to develop compassion as we broaden our perception of life, and everything in it. The world becomes more than just our personal experience. We begin to understand the nature of shared experience, and to understand the reality of this shared experience. By being mindful, we are fully present in the moment of that shared experience, and by virtue of that fact we see more clearly.

With the earth fully awake now, we can hear the songs of others even as we ourselves sing. We learn to find our place in our environment, and work in harmony to nourish and sustain the whole for the betterment of all. Seeing with the eyes of compassion helps us to achieve this, and following Right View allows the beauty of reality to seep into every aspect of our daily lives.

Problems arise when our perceptions of reality become twisted with the imaginative and creative thought processes that our human brains are so capable of. Stories change with the telling; we know this. But we are fooling ourselves when we keep changing reality to suit our own egos and emotions. We have to learn how to live in the here and now. Being alive and present in the here and now allows no time for emotional attachment to our thoughts and feelings; we still respond emotionally to situations, but we don't become attached to the emotion itself. Let us continue to tell stories, for we are a storytelling species, but let us not live in a made-up world that we have created in our minds.

Look deeply into the story that you have created of your own life. If someone else were telling the tale, how would it differ? Would their point of view be less valid? Do we create drama unnecessarily, do others? Does this give us attention when we do, does it add flavour or spice to what we might consider an otherwise dull existence? Our own lives are brilliant and fascinating enough, we don't need to add more drama to them. By doing so, we will miss our own lives, living instead in our minds and foregoing some of the wondrous nature that is constantly unfolding right before our very eyes. We can hurt other people by making up stories to suit our egos and our needs, but the person whom we hurt most is ourselves.

At Beltane, we begin with Right View to let go of the representational ego, to allow a deeper integration without giving up the functional self that gets things done. This means that we do things, but aren't overly concerned with any attention we receive because of it, or any reward for instance. This is just one example; there are many ways open to us when we begin to delve deeply into the ego. Zen Buddhism is all about letting go of the ego so that we understand each other better, where the illusion of the Self and the Other have fallen away and all that remains is shared experience. This is Right View.

Go for a walk. When walking, do so in a meditative state, as at Imbolc when we first learned walking meditation. Open up to a wider sense of perception by allowing your sense of self to fall away. Widen the circle of your identity to include your environment, and see how that makes you feel. Are you walking differently? Do not judge, simply walk and allow yourself to flow with your surroundings, knowing that you are a part of the ecosystem. If you become distracted by thoughts or judgements, breathe deeply and let them go, once again widening your sense of perception. You can even try to let go of your focus and begin to work with peripheral vision. Experiment with walking without focusing (as long as it is safe) and by using your peripheral vision. Stop the thinking self and look with more than your eyes, if you can. See with your belly, with your feet.

In the growing light, with the energy rising, we can work deeply with perception for the benefit of all, not just ourselves. We take the seeds that we have planted and watch over them, nurturing and caring for them. We pay attention to the environment and acknowledge the life force that is existent within all things. We begin to see that the barrier between ourselves and the rest of the world is just an illusion, and we perceive reality clearly with the eyes of compassion.

Things to do from Beltane to Summer Solstice:

- Meditate outside. Feel the rising energy of the earth.
- Define for yourself the essence of compassion. Read articles, watch videos, get different perspectives. A good starting point is Thich Nhat Hanh's book, *True Love*. (See bibliography for more.)
- Review the Four Noble Truths. Look at them in your personal life, then extend them to your family, your friends, ever widening the circle until you can understand them in relation to the world on a deep and intimate level.

- Continue with the walking meditation first described at Imbolc. Walk with a deep shared experience with the rest of the nature, with the rest of the world. Open up to your peripheral senses. Expand your vision. Let go.
- Research the fire aspect of this festival. See fire as a tool of transformation. Understand how fire can help or hinder, can nourish or destroy. Compare fire with your notion of yourself, with your ego. Try some exercises where in meditation you feed your representational ego, where you allow your mind to run away with inflated thoughts of yourself. Now do the same with deflating thoughts. Finally, allow that sense of self to fall away, and find deep integration in that letting go. Try to carry that sense of letting go into the wider perspective with you throughout the day.
- Remind yourself of the seeds that you have planted, and look at them with Right View. Do they need any adjustment? Do they require any special attention? Nourish those seeds carefully, watering them with your focus.

Chapter Eleven

Summer Solstice

The sun has reached its peak height, and the longest day of the year has arrived. It's time to celebrate!

Extract from *Zen Druidry: Living a Natural Life with Full Awareness* by Joanna van der Hoeven:

> *At Midsummer, or the Summer Solstice, we revel in the time of longest light, the days seem to linger forever, the twilight hours bringing cool release from the heat of the day, and the very short nights give way to early dawn. The sun is at its peak, and so too can we feel the same way at this time of year. Honouring the cycle of the sun is important in Druidry, and reflecting the times and tides back so that we can better attune ourselves to the world around us is all important. This is also a challenging time, for those sensitive to the light, or heat; it is a time for the making or breaking of a soul, much like the Winter Solstice. This is the time for Right Action, for at the height of our powers we should act responsibly.*

The longest day is, in a northerly region such as the British Isles, a cause for celebration. The warm sun bestows its blessings upon us (if we're lucky) and, as mostly diurnal creatures, we enjoy this prolonged sunlight. Many people feel at the height of their power at this time of year, filled with the energy of the sun. For others, this time of year is a difficult one, when retreat into the cool darkness is preferred and the quiet of the Winter Solstice seems a haven of refuge that is so far away. No matter which you prefer, the darkness or the light, both the solstices are times to celebrate the highest and lowest points in the solar year in equal measure. We welcome the light and the dark equally as powers of nature that flow through us and the land.

As we saw with the Winter Solstice, there are many sacred Neolithic sites around Britain that are aligned with the solstices. Many of them also record the rising of the moon at certain times of the year, such as at Stonehenge where once (before the stones fell) one was able to view the midwinter setting sun and the new moon's crescent every so often between the stones. We still are able to view the Summer Solstice sunrise, however, from the Heel Stone (from the Old Welsh *haul:* pertaining to the sun). Indeed, at Stonehenge after much controversy in the 1980s, there is a public celebration of the Summer Solstice each year, when free access is granted for all those who wish to view the spectacle from the stones which are otherwise cordoned off the rest of the year (special access permits can be obtained from English Heritage, at a small cost for those who wish private use of the stones for ritual, meditation, etc.). Sadly, this has resulted in much litter being left behind by people not attuned to the sacredness of the site, who merely wish to 'party' in the stones all night. It would be unthinkable behaviour, say, in Chartres Cathedral, yet somehow it happens within the stones of Stonehenge, with people climbing on the stones, shouting and drumming their victory. While spiritual ecstasy and letting go are an essential part of any earth-based tradition, bad behaviour is not, and care must be taken to preserve our ancient sites.

And so we look to Right Action at this time of year, when at the height of the sun's power, its rays illuminating all that we do, we ensure that our actions are honourable. The spotlight is on us, especially as Druids in the United Kingdom, with the usual media frenzy that this time of year brings. Let us look to our actions and behaviour and be an example, be the light that we wish to see in the world. It is a time of great responsibility (as all times are) when self-interest is exchanged for compassion and integration with the world. Sincerity and honesty are paramount, both to ourselves and to the world we live in. We cannot hide in the shadows at the time of greatest light. Right Action means working in any environment in a way that is harmonious, that benefits the whole rather than the one.

We understand the illusion of separation and we work to move beyond that, into utter integration with the natural world. We use our wisdom and compassion to help us work in the world. Through mindfulness of our words, thoughts and deeds we learn deeply about our own behaviour, and change it accordingly so that we are in tune with the nature of the whole, as we know that we are a part of that whole. We know that when we litter, we are throwing rubbish onto our home. When we speak ill of others, we are speaking ill of ourselves. When we consume too much, we are taking from others who are in need and our own future ancestors (essentially, ourselves).

Now is the time to shine that summer light upon your soul, upon your sense of self. What could you do that would benefit the whole? What actions can you take to change your behaviour, should it need changing? None of us are perfect, and we can always work on ourselves and our behaviour in order to find balance and harmony. Do you gossip at work about other colleagues? Then you must remember Right Speech, and take Right Action to stop it. Do you watch too much television? Then you must remember Right View, and take Right Action to help you return to what really matters in life, to living in the moment, to the wonders of reality in the present moment. Do you harbour anger or jealousy towards another person? Then we must remember Right Intention, and with Right Action water the seeds of love and compassion rather than anger or jealousy. There are stories that we are not aware of within each and every person we meet, and simply focusing on angry or jealous feelings towards that person is not seeing with the eyes of compassion, not working with the whole. Right action means that we work closely with Right Effort to really make the changes we need in our lives to help end suffering, both within and without.

Many in Buddhism see Right Action as really embodying the

Five Precepts, which again are:

1. Refrain from killing living beings
2. Refrain from taking that which is not given
3. Refrain from sexual misconduct
4. Refrain from false speech/gossip
5. Refrain from intoxicants

It's time to shine that spotlight from our nearest star on our behaviour. We can work with the energy of the sun at its highest point to make the changes we wish to see. We look at our jobs, our diets, our consumption of resources and relate that to the first precept. We look at feelings of envy, jealousy, covetousness in our lives, and work to let them go in relation to the second precept. We do not take for granted our lovers and partners, and maintain the sacredness of sexual union in the third precept. We know the power of words, their meaning, and watch our speech, instead speaking with kindness and empathy, encouragement and love with regards to the fourth precept. We look at all that we consume, especially intoxicants, and realise that we are what we take into our bodies and our minds in relation to the fifth precept. We look at the seeds we planted in the spring, and ensure that they are well looked after, nourished with only the best that we can offer.

When our energy is at its peak, we are reminded of our ethics. To live with a sense of honour and integrity, we must first establish our own ethics as Druids and/or Buddhists. We keep in mind the widened perception of the whole, rather than just our own part in life with regards to everything that we do. Consider deeply the nature of ethical behaviour, of your personal and of global ethics. Where do they differ? How can you work in the world to achieve balance and peace? How can you work for the betterment of the whole, rather than the one? Consider these questions deeply in meditation, and let the time of highest light guide you into the change you wish to see in the world.

Things to do from the Summer Solstice to Lughnasadh:

- Look deeply at the Five Precepts with regards to your way of life.
- Meditate and explore aspects of your behaviour that you feel you can improve upon. Go outside into the sunlight and soak in the sun's rays (with proper protection) and allow that energy to fuel you in your quest.
- Develop you own set of ethics that you wish to live by, keeping in mind the sum of the whole rather than the parts. Here is an example by Canadian musician Loreena McKennitt, from her biographical web page at http://loreenamckennitt.com/about/.

  - Be compassionate and never forget how to love.
  - Think inclusively.
  - Reclaim noble values such as truth, honesty, honour, courage.
  - Respect one's elders and look to what they have to teach you.
  - Be empathetic.
  - Look after the less fortunate in society.
  - Promote and protect diversity.
  - Respect the gifts of the natural world.
  - Set your goals high and take pride in what you do.
  - Cherish and look after your body, and, as the ancient Greeks believed, your mind will serve you better.
  - Put back into the community as there have been those before you who have done the same and you are reaping what they sowed.
  - Participate in and protect democracy. It does not thrive as a spectator sport.
  - Undertake due diligence in everything.

- Seek balance and space, and solitude.
- Don't be afraid to feel passionate about something.
- Learn to be an advocate and an ambassador for good.
- Be mindful of your limitations.
- Indulge and nurture your curiosity as it will keep you vital.
- Take charge of your life and don't fall into the pit of entitlement.
- Assume nothing and take nothing for granted.
- Things are not necessarily what they seem.

• After considering your own behaviour, consider the behaviour of others towards you, especially the nature of revenge. What are the repercussions?
• Consider the word 'responsibility', being the ability to respond.
• How can you be the change you wish to see in the world? Do it.
• What seeds did you plant in the spring? What can you offer to them, with full honour and integrity, at this time of year? How can you harness the power of the sun to help them come to their full potential?

Chapter Twelve

Lughnasadh

The first grain harvest is in, and we celebrate its bounty. The summer days are still long, and we work/celebrate in equal measure through the dog days of summer.

Extract from *Zen Druidry: Living a Natural Life with Full Awareness* by Joanna van der Hoeven:

> *At the beginning of August is Lughnasadh, or Lammas, the celebration of the cutting of the first grain crop. It is a time to see the product of our work since the long dreaming and introspection of winter. If we have worked hard, and external factors beyond our control (and nothing is ever under our total control) have been beneficial to our plans, then what we have sown in the spring should now start to come to fruition. The flowers are out in full force, the trees swaying in the breeze, and the long dog days of August lie ahead. There is no time to stop; we must still keep at our work for our harvest to be fruitful. It is a time for exchange and trade as well, for at this time our ancestors gathered to celebrate the first harvest with festivals honouring not only the time of year, but also to honour community and family. Love that bloomed in the spring came to marriage in August, vows were exchanged, goods and labour agreed upon. The time for Right Speech falls into this tide neatly; words have power, words have weight.*

Lughnasadh (pronounced loo-na-sah) marks the beginning of the harvest season. It is another one of the four seasonal, agricultural or fire festivals in the Wheel of the Year, focusing on changes in the land, rather than astronomical events (though some people use the nearest full moon to mark these seasonal festivals). The hard work that we have put in over the spring and summer is beginning to come into fruition, and we will have an idea as to whether our crop will be bountiful or not. The traditional tale of John Barleycorn is often sung, as we honour the nourishment even as we honour the death that brings nourishment. It is a stressful time for modern-day farmers still, hoping to get their crops in before it rains. Often you can hear the combine harvesters working deep into the night as news of an impending storm hits (and most combine harvesters are rented by the day in the UK). It was a time of celebration as well, with the weeks leading up to the harvest filled with contests and games, horse races being prominent. Most especially, wedding vows were spoken at this time as well as trade exchanges. Honouring of your word is an all-important part of this festival.

In our digital age, using Right Speech becomes all the more relevant. Without the benefit of human contact, words exchanged can change in their meaning, or the self becomes far too involved in sustaining its own egoistic nature. If we look to the Buddha's teachings on Right Speech, and consider how quickly information has developed over the past few years, we can see that perhaps we as humans have not quite been able to catch up to the technology in order to express our ideas with absolute integrity, honesty or compassion.

We are expressive creatures. We are vocal, and exchange our ideas mostly through speaking. Up until recently we communicated through face-to-face interaction or through hand-written letters. We need to relearn the value and importance of words and their meaning, taking our time and really thinking about what is coming out of our mouths or minds before we communicate them in whatever form we choose. We all know the old saying: 'The pen is mightier than the sword.' Words can inspire or destroy. When we are mindful with words, we begin to truly understand the meaning of compassion and peace.

First we begin with silence. It may seem contradictory, but the intention will become clear. When we learn the value of silence, and we have begun to still the chattering of our minds, then we are better able to think clearly, listen more closely without judgement and really be in the present moment. When we operate in the present moment, instead of being influenced by past troubles or future worries, then we are best able to respond; we are practising true responsibility. We have worked with responsibility at the Summer Solstice, and now we begin to see how that reflects in all aspects of our lives. To further our ability to respond, we work with deep silence in order to hear the stories of others. In hearing the stories of others, we lessen the importance of the story of ourselves and begin to find our place in the whole. We begin to work with the ego in stillness and silence.

When we have worked with silence, we learn the value of communication. We understand the importance of words. We can see how much words and communication are taken for granted in today's society, and how much they are twisted to represent a particular point of view, one that is usually self-affirming or self-aggrandizing for whatever reason: money, power, ego and so on. We begin to look deeply into our modes of communication, and the words that we use to communicate with others. Do we have ulterior motives? Are those motives honourable? Are they compassionate? Do they work for the benefit of the whole, or are they self-serving?

We learn that idle chatter is a waste of time. We learn that abusive speech hurts ourselves as much as it hurts others. When we speak ill of others, we speak ill of ourselves, for we are all inter-related. People may hurt us, but is hurting them in return really the path forward to a life of less suffering? Use the tools of communication to spread peace rather than wage war. You have every right to stand up for what you believe in, as long as you do it with honour, integrity and compassion. Speak out with Right Speech.

Politicians live by the power of words. Yet most of them are not the best examples, though there are one or two out there who really do live up to their honour and ideals. The media are a huge influence on everything that happens around us. Yet when we cut through all the chatter and insults, the lies and the ulterior motives, we move into a place of stillness where what matters most is what we do, not what we say. In this context, the word Druid here is not a noun: it is a verb.

When we consider the sum of the whole, rather than its parts in everything that we do, then we are Druid. When we see the bigger picture, and realise that life is not just our own journey, but that of many others' songs flowing into one brilliant chorus, then we are Druid. When we learn, when we teach, when we seek soul-to-soul relationship with the blackbird, the cycles of the sun and moon, the forest or human nature, then we are Druid. Druid is not what you say. Druid is what you do.

As such, Druidry is a way of life, and not a religion or spirituality to be practised once a week, or at a set time each day. Druidry is everything that you do, from washing up the dishes with an eco-friendly dish soap to installing solar panels on your roof. It is about making choices and acting upon them, bearing in mind the entirety of the natural world and the consequences of your actions. It is taking a close look at your modes of consumerism and of expenditure. It is about deep thinking, critical analysis and heart-wrenching emotion. It is about ecstasy and the mundane.

So, though we use words to communicate, we do not use them heedlessly, recklessly or without purpose. We blend the teachings of Right Speech with Right Action to truly live our Druidry, to bring it to life with purpose and integrity.

Wedding vows were often spoken by our ancestors at this time of year. It is a good reminder for us to look at what promises we make, as well as the words we use. Do we walk our talk? If not, why not? What is holding us back? If we think of words as commitments, then we will use them more wisely.

The seeds of your intention are ripening under the summer

sun. Will you hold true to the commitment you made when you planted it in the spring? Will you keep to your word? The Harvest Home, the Autumn Equinox, will soon be upon us, and we will truly reap what we sow.

Things to think about from Lughnasadh to the Autumn Equinox:

- Try a day without speech or communication in verbal or written form, if you can. If that is impossible, try maybe a couple of hours, or an hour, without media input or personal output from yourself. Spend some time in quiet stillness, letting words and thoughts go for however long a time. Simply learn how to be without words.

- Take a good, hard look at the forms of communication that you use. Are they beneficial? Are they a waste of time? How much of it is idle chatter? How could that time be better spent?

- Go outside to a field of barley or wheat, if you can. Spend some time with the golden stalks of grain, feeling the energy of the land, the potential shimmering in the sunshine. After the harvest, go back to that field and sit again with the land, connecting with it and feeling any changes. Sing back to the land.

- Handwrite a letter to a family member, or to a close friend. How do your words differ than if you were communicating via telephone, or social media? How does it make you feel to spend time writing a letter? Having to wait to mail it, and then awaiting a response?

- Have you kept to the seeds of intention that you planted at spring? Have you kept your word? If not, how can you rectify or salvage it before the harvest at the Autumn Equinox?

Chapter Thirteen

Autumn Equinox

The harvest has well and truly arrived, and we are hard at work reaping all that we have sown. We see the fruits of our labours and celebrate the bounty.

Extract from *Zen Druidry: Living a Natural Life with Full Awareness* by Joanna van der Hoeven:

The Autumn Equinox brings us again to that point of balance where we wait upon the edge for the tide to turn fully to the dark half of the year, where the nights become longer than the days. The leaves are beginning to change, the nights are chill and the best of the flowers have gone. Nature is slowly winding down, animals are beginning their migrations. The tractors and combine harvesters are out in full force, gathering the crops of onions, turnips and corn. The deer are beginning to come together in larger herds for the winter; all are making preparations for the colder months. Our ancestors did as much as they could to prepare for the winter, and so too should we, even in our much easier, softer existence. This is the time for Right Livelihood, ensuring that what we do for a living is compassionate, and does not abuse others or the environment. Our ancestors needed to come together at this time of year to ensure they made it through the dark days of winter, so too must we come together to see that the impact that we make upon this planet, our home, is for the benefit of all, and not just the few, or our own selves.

We stand once more on the knife's edge, balanced between light and darkness. At the Autumn Equinox, we fall over the tipping point into darkness, where the nights are longer than the days. For a brief moment all is held in balance, day and night are equal, and then we begin the descent into the long nights of winter. At this balance point, just as at the Spring Equinox, there is great power and opportunity. We welcome the light and dark parts of the year equally, for we know that darkness is as much a blessing as light. In darkness, there is rest and respite, where boundaries and edges fall away. We can work to let go of our egos when we work with the darkness, learning how to integrate when the edges are softened and the nourishment of darkness fills our heart and souls. Just as a seed needs darkness before germinating, so too do we need darkness to help us continue in the cycles of life, death and regeneration.

When we work with darkness, we see that the importance of the self is vastly over-rated. Knowing that we are part of an ecosystem, part of our environment, our own sense of self-importance fades away in the lengthening nights. We understand that what is important is the whole, not the one. We learn about service.

Druidry is all about service: service to the land, the gods and the ancestors. It is not just for ourselves. We live in reverence to the natural world, and in our reverence we find a way to work within its cycles to benefit the whole. We learn about responsibility, and understand our duty as what we owe to the world that nourishes and sustains us day after day, night after night. We find perfect freedom in service, for our egos take a back seat and we can truly live, experience, work and love without all the sticky judgements and pronouncements from the ego. We are not burdened by our responsibilities, but rather see them as the doorways to freedom.

Druidry can be summed up in three words: truth, honour and service. Yet these words can be very vague. What do they mean to the Druid?

Truth is not just figurative and literal truth. There are other dimensions to the word when we see it in accordance with our views of the world and religion or spirituality. Druids have a deep reverence for nature, connecting to the world through awen, the flowing inspiration that guides and directs and that is each entity's own soul song. When each thing is living in accordance with its own soul song, in accordance with its own nature, in accordance with nature as a whole, then it is following its own truth.

The world around us tries to muddy the waters of our truth, making us believe we need more than we could possibly know what to do with, making us think we are above others, making us feel inferior, unworthy and unloved. It tries to tell us that we are lacking. When we take a step back away from the world, we can examine it from a different perspective, seeing what is often termed in Druidry as 'the truth against the world'.

This truth is our soul song. It shines from us when we live in accordance with nature. It flows like the awen when we care for ourselves, others and the planet. It springs forth when we acknowledge the times and tides of life and death. When we step away from what really matters, from living our own truth, we can feel distanced from the world and from each other, and perhaps even our own selves. We must return to the basics of what is our place is within nature, and how we can live in harmony and balance with it. When we do, we are then living our truth.

Honour is another word that lies in the hazy mists of time. It has connotations of chivalry, fealty and nobility. Yet honour is simply the courage to live our soul truth in the world. It is standing strong by our principles of balance and harmony, making the world better for all. Returning again to what really matters, to our place in the world, is at the heart of honour. It is not a one-time thing that we can achieve and then sit back, resting on our laurels. Honour requires hard work, all the time, to see that we are indeed living our soul truths to the best of our ability.

When we come to understand truth and honour, the natural outcome is service. We live our lives in service to our Druidry –

we can do no other. We are not subservient to anyone but ourselves. Living in accordance with our own nature, our own truths and finding sustainability through honour, it naturally results in service to the world, that same world that tries to rail against our truth! The cycle is ever flowing, and we work in service to the truth and the world in equal measure. That is where we find the most balance and harmony. That is what makes it so special, as well as bloody hard work sometimes.

Truth. Honour. Service. Three words; three concepts, a triad inextricably linked together, like beautiful Celtic knotwork.

Right Livelihood fits in perfectly with this concept of living in service, for all that we do is a reflection of our Druidry. As stated previously in this text, Druid is a verb as well as a noun. Druidry is what you do, not what you say. So, in order for your Druidry to be sincere, you must walk the talk. You must live in harmony with the natural cycle, and not just read about it or only show up to the eight celebrations in the year. It is living moment to moment in full awareness.

Right Livelihood is mainly considered to be the work that you do, as in your job and income, however, it extends beyond that into everything you do. Certainly, we must ensure that how we make our income is honourable and we can always find ways to work in harmony. If we have a job that doesn't, we can put our effort into finding a new one. In Druidry, we always have a choice. It is in the making of this choice, and the integrity to live honourably by our choices, that determines who and what we are. It is living an honourable life. It is being Druid.

Things to do from the Autumn Equinox to Samhain:

- Meditate upon truth, honour and service. What do those words mean to you? Write down any feelings you might have, and review them at a later date. Have they changed? Deepened or grown?
- Look at the responsibilities in your life. How do you see

them? Are they merely obligations? Are they burdens? Or are they gifts? Do you provide care for a loved one? See that as a gift, not a chore. Look deeply into your responsibilities, and meditate upon the meaning of the words: *response* and *ability*.

- Look at the work that provides you with an income, or sustenance of any form. Is it in tune with the benefit of the whole? Does it fall within the concept of Right Livelihood? If not, what changes can you make to align yourself more fully with Right Livelihood?

- The days will now tip over into darkness: How can darkness be worked with? Who are the gods of darkness?

- Sit outside (in a safe place) at twilight and see how the edges are softened until all is merged into one. Let that inspire you on your journey through the dark days of the coming winter. Learn the night sky; learn about your home environment after dark.

- You have now harvested from the seeds of your intention that you cared for throughout the year. These seeds have grown, and will provide you with nourishment throughout the long winter. They also provide the seeds for next year. As you reap what you have sown, begin to think about what you will keep with you as you approach Samhain, the cycle beginning again.

Part Three – Meditation

Meditation is at the heart of Zen. Zazen literally means meditation. In zazen, we perform sitting meditation, where we rest the body and the mind for a period of time in order to experience reality, living in the present moment. When we exist in the present moment we are free, we are enlightened. We are no longer burdened by the past or troubled about the future; there exists only this moment, right now.

Meditation is a tool to help us get to that state so that we can carry the present moment with us in everything that we do, from rising out of the bed in the morning to sitting on the bus, walking up a stairway at work, eating out with friends or celebrating with family. When we set aside time each day for meditation, we are practising being in the present moment. The more we practise, the better we become at it and the easier it will be to find that inner peace and contentment that we often find lacking in our lives. Using mindfulness we hone our skill, addressing issues that need further exploration simply by being in the present moment.

Meditation is an important part of the Druid tradition as well. Many see meditation and prayer going hand in hand, for prayer is communicating with the divine, or the ancestors, or the spirits of place, and meditation is listening for the answer. When we find stillness, when silence fills our souls, then we are better able to hear the songs of nature all around us. When we are at peace with ourselves, we are at peace with the world. As the Druid strives to work in balance and harmony with the natural world, honouring it for all that it is, meditation can become the heart of the tradition as well.

It is important to quiet our chattering minds. We run a constant narrative, most of us, throughout every waking second of our lives. It can be utterly exhausting. We can fabricate entire scenarios and situations in our minds while we should be paying attention to things like driving a car, or taking a shower, making a cup of tea. We can become so lost in the convoluted twists of our minds that we live entirely in our heads, and the real world passes us by. What a waste that would be!

When our minds become quiet, we are better able to perceive the world as it truly is, rather than how we think it should be. We begin to let go of our perception of the world, and realise that there is no one right or wrong view: simply many views. We let go of dualistic thinking and begin to realise that each perception can be tightly held onto with judgements, which will only cause division and separation. When we extend our perception, we begin to see the whole, rather than a part of the picture. When we don't attach to our perception; it widens out so that it grasps the entirety. Instead of seeing through a pinhole, we are treated to an enormous panoramic view.

Chapter Fourteen

Mindtraps

Every day we are caught in mindtraps, those little prisons of our own making. We are constantly hijacked by our thoughts and feelings, attachments to them and our egos, such that we spin endlessly in circles until we fall down. The key to breaking free of these mindtraps is through observation and meditation.

When we meditate in the Zen style, we become aware of our bodies and our thoughts. We do not 'zone out', we are not 'away with the faeries' or pondering the mysteries of life; in zazen we focus on pure experience. This focus helps us in our lives when we are not in zazen. We are aware of how our bodies are feeling: whether our breath is shallow or deep, that twinge in our back, whether our facial muscles are tense or relaxed. We also turn that awareness to our surroundings, listening to the birdsong outside, or the traffic, feeling the breeze or the sunlight upon our shoulders. We are aware as much as is humanly possible of everything that is around us and within us. It is no easy task.

Our thoughts are constantly seeking to distract us from the comfortable reality that we have created. Even though this reality may be a false reality, still it is more comfortable than sitting, thinking about our headache or the plain 'boredom' of doing zazen. We daydream, we think through all our life's problems, we spin off in attempts to do anything but simply be in the moment, because we feel that we deserve otherwise. Remember that old saying, 'there is no time like the present'? Similarly, there is no real experience other than this present moment. Perhaps the best thing you could be doing is simply experiencing the present moment as it is, right now.

We like to think. There is nothing wrong with thinking; we can solve problems and work out situations with a little forethought.

We plan; there is nothing wrong with having life plans. It is our attachment to these plans that sets us off in another mindtrap, where if we don't achieve them our life can feel in ruins.

In zazen, we learn to observe. We sit, and we observe our body's attempts to defy our intention of just sitting still and being in the moment. Why do our bodies do this? Because they reflect our thoughts; our thoughts don't want to sit still, they want to run riot. In zazen it is not so much controlling our thoughts, pushing them away or yelling at them to be quiet like unruly children; rather we observe the thoughts and gradually, through observing them, they become quieter. A new thought is a wonderful, shiny thing that we want to explore, whether it is a 'good' thought or a 'bad' thought. When we have observed that thought 100 times, it becomes a lot less interesting. This is what zazen is about.

If we think about what happened to us that may have upset us during the day, we can easily become lost in our emotional attachment to it. If we simply observe the thought by saying: 'Oh, I'm having a thought about this again,' we can then return our attention to simply sitting and being in the moment, and we are on the path to freedom from these mindtraps. Again, it is not easy; we may have to do this 10, 100 or 1,000 times before the thoughts settle down and we tire of them. With persistence, they will.

We must be careful, however, to simply observe, without 'being' the observer. If we become the observer, then we have created a separate entity that does not exist. If we are simply observing, then we are the pure moment. The past does not exist, neither does the future. It is only this moment, that is constantly changing, that exists. If thoughts about the past occur, you can observe them, but then ask yourself: 'Where is the past right now?' It does not exist. When we worry about the future, we can ask our self: 'Where is the future right now?' It does not exist. Only this present, ever-changing moment exists.

I love to daydream, but not when I am in meditation. I set

aside a time in the day to daydream, to come up with wonderful stories that may see the light of day in future novels or short stories. There is nothing wrong with imagination; it is a gift that should be used every day. We must learn, however, not to become lost in it, this imaginary world, as it can seem so much better than our reality. Living in a pure moment does not leave us as unthinking, mindless zombies. We are totally and completely present, truly living life to the fullest. That is the greatest gift.

It is time to break free of your mindtraps. Look at what thoughts keep occurring, what keeps rising to the surface when you are being silent and still. By observing them you will notice them, notice the patterns that are created, the emotions and physical pain that may be attached to these thoughts and how they so easily control your life. Once we see the pattern, we can weave our way out into a new pattern, into a new cycle. Through zazen, we can take this into our everyday lives, and so, when someone upsets us, or hurts us, or brings us joy we can see the pattern that is created and either choose to remain within it, or weave a new pattern upon the web of life. We can either live in this very moment, or stay within our mindtraps. The choice is ours.

Author's personal perspective and experience with meditation

Meditation is a huge part of my spiritual life. It is something that I try to do every single day, in various shapes and forms. I find that sitting meditation, or zazen, is the best way for me to refocus on what's important, to stop the chattering ego and really get deep down to the issues at hand. So much clarity is gained from simply stopping, from allowing the silence to fill your soul. In the deep pool of meditative quiet, in the dark heart of Cerridwen's cauldron, lies transformation.

You have to be willing to do it, though. It's difficult, as many of us don't really like spending time alone, much less sitting still and 'wasting time'. However, I would posit that this could very well be the best use of your time, realigning you to the present moment, grounding yourself in the reality of the here and now. We can get so carried away on our emotions, on our problems with the world, on our own sense of self that we become blinkered to the rest of existence. Life is constantly happening, all around us, and we hardly notice it. Sitting meditation is a great way to pay attention to it, to ourselves, our bodies and our minds, to see how they work, to get in touch with them once again, thereby allowing us to get in touch with the rest of the world on a much clearer, positive level.

Like a deep pool, the waters may become disturbed, but if we stop the mud will eventually settle to the bottom, the clear water rising to the top to perfectly reflect the sky above. We can become as this pool, reflecting with clarity the present moment in all that we do, in all that we say and in all that we think. It's not easy, but it's well worth it.

It takes a lot of practise. A lot. I can guarantee you won't get the hang of it if you only try for a couple of days and then give up, saying, 'I can't do it.' Perhaps 'can't' isn't the issue, but rather 'won't'. We have to be willing to step up the challenge, to breathe in the silence and face the abyss. Perhaps this is too frightening for some, facing who they really are, seeing their actions and their behaviour in the clear reflective pool of being. For others, it's an opportunity for growth, to not let ourselves be slaves to our shadow selves, that which lurks beneath our perception. When our shadow selves rule, we live reactionary lives (lives led only by reacting to situations, instead of acting with intention). When we are unaware, life slips past us at an alarming rate. Things often seem out of control. We then release all personal responsibility; we simply quit, saying, 'I can't do this.'

Meditation can be your personal cheerleader. It can discipline the body and the mind, saying, 'Yes, you can, just do it!' In times of great trauma, in times of great stress, meditation will allow you to transition these moments into ones of mindfulness, wisdom and ultimately joy. When we are kind to ourselves, through quiet meditation, breathing in to our souls, breathing in to our hearts, our lungs, our ancestors, our gods then we create joy, both within and without. Meditation is all about having compassion for yourself.

Try it, if you don't already incorporate meditation into your daily schedule. Simply find time to sit for 15-20 minutes, either on a cushion on the floor, or a chair. If sitting is just too uncomfortable, due to illness or injury, then lying down is fine as long as you won't fall asleep. There are many different meditation positions that you can try out to find the one that is most suitable. Take a few moments to allow your body to rest comfortably into position. Your spine should be straight and relaxed. If sitting on a chair, try not to use the backrest. If sitting on the floor, try using cushions to raise your seat slightly off the floor, so that when you sit 'cross-legged' your hips will be the same height or higher than your knees. I bring my right foot in first, and then have the left leg in front of that; the legs are not 'crossed' but rather folded inwards, as depicted in the Gundestrup cauldron artefact now famous in Celtic archaeology. A similar position is also sometimes referred to as the Burmese position in Zen Buddhist meditation. With legs folded inwards instead of being crossed, the circulation still flows freely. If I do cross my legs, one of them falls asleep.

I then rest my hands on my knees, palms down, bringing my elbows back slightly if I find I am leaning too far forwards. I rock back and forth a bit to find the centre spot on my seat bones, and then close my eyes, focusing on my breath. After years of practise, I can now usually focus on the breath straight away without thoughts of the day, past experience or future worries crowding in. If you find this happening, simply smile, let it go and return your focus to the breath. Try this for just 10 minutes. You may have to refocus 10, 20, 100 times, but each time simply smile to your mind and return to your breath. It's not about how good you are at focusing, but about coming to an understanding about how your mind works. Once you see how often these thoughts come in, and how often you have to let go, you will realise how much these thoughts have controlled you. It's time to take charge now, and let them go with a smile.

The last five minutes of my meditation session are filled with prayer. If you like, you can always begin with prayer, and then meditate afterwards. I do this if there is an issue or a question that I need to look deeper into, questing inspiration. Then, the meditation is opening yourself up to receiving an answer, by turning off the chatter and allowing the gods or ancestors to speak in the newly found silence.

Build up the sessions until you can do 20-45 minutes a day. You may find that your back muscles ache from sitting upright after two minutes, that's fine, they probably haven't been used very much and just need time to strengthen. Holding in the lower belly a little helps, as long as it doesn't restrict your breathing. Gradually, you will find your back muscles getting stronger, and you will be able to sit in position for longer periods of time. Stick with it.

When the body and mind are stilled, we return to ourselves. In the stillness of the centre, we can see the world around us. Let that world spin, for it will go on regardless; know that here at the centre, in the present moment, there is only the stillness, the silence and the breath. How exquisite a gift!

Chapter Fifteen

Preparation, Posture and Basic Meditation

Preparation

It is a good idea to create a place of peace where you can perform your meditation. Many Druids have altars in or around their homes at which they make offerings, meditate, pray and so on. If you have a spare room, that is an excellent place to create a little sanctuary. You can also create a space in a corner of your bedroom, or even a pop-up area in your living room that you can take down afterwards to save it from young children and/or pets. What matters most is that it is pleasing to you. It is best to start indoors, mastering the art of meditation before taking it to an outside altar, as there can be many more distractions when out of doors. You can burn candles as a focal point for your meditation, as well as incense or fragrant oils. Keep your altar clean and fairly neat; it doesn't have to be pristine, but gathering dust and old food from offerings or dirty water in a flower vase is not very conducive to creating the kind of atmosphere we want in meditation. We want our meditation to help us be fresh, peaceful and relaxed. Ensure that all distractions are taken care of: take the phone off the hook or turn it off and tell family/household members that you are to be left undisturbed. You can take off your shoes and leave them by the door, to indicate that you wish some quiet meditation time.

It is best to try to meditate at the same time each day. This does not have to be by the clock; you can meditate at sunrise and sunset each day. Try to meditate at least once a day. Begin slowly, with a five or 10-minute meditation, and slowly work up to 20 minutes or more. Quality, not quantity, is what matters most. If you can really focus and be still for five minutes, that is better than sitting for 30 minutes with a wandering mind.

Ensure that clothing is not restrictive. You do not want to wear anything with a tight waistband, for example. You will want to be able to breathe freely, and sit relaxed without any constricting items of clothing. Take your shoes off. Ensure that you will be warm or cool enough.

Basic posture

So we begin by sitting down, in a comfortable position. It can be cross-legged on a cushion on the floor, or first folding in one leg, then the other, sitting in half-lotus (one foot on the opposite thigh) or full lotus (both feet resting upon the opposite thigh). Half lotus and full lotus require quite a degree of flexibility, so please be careful attempting these poses. You do not want to do yourself an injury by meditating! You can also sit on a chair if that is more comfortable. Do not force your body into a position. Meditative poses such as half lotus and full lotus require a lot of flexibility in the knees, ankles and hips. Meditation should be comfortable.

If sitting on the floor, ensure that your seat is lifted high enough so that your knees are in line or lower than your hips. This will stabilise you, and also ensure that your circulation will not be compromised. Rock back and forth a few times, to settle your seat bones on your cushion, and place your hands on your thighs, near your knees, palms down to begin with. Roll your shoulders back and let the shoulder blades relax down your back. Sit with a straight back, envisioning a line pulling your spine upright until it floats gently into position. Keeping your shoulders back, allow your shoulder blades to relax down your spine. Tilt your chin slightly downwards to elongate the spine at the neck and base of the head.

If you are sitting on a chair, ensure that both feet are comfortably flat on the floor (you may need to raise them on a cushion) and sit forwards, not using the backrest. Float the spine upwards and tilt the chin downwards slightly. Roll the shoulders back, and rest your hands on your thighs.

Basic meditation: Zazen or mindfulness meditation (around 10 minutes)

The meditation below is an aid to help you get to a place of stillness.

Shift your gaze slightly downwards, soften the focus of the eyes, and begin.

Become aware of your breath. Don't try to change it for now, simply be aware of your breath, whether it is deep and slow, or shallow and fast. Try to breathe through your nose, if at all possible. Feel the chest rise and fall with each inhale and exhale. Feel the stomach expanding upon inhalation, and falling back towards your spine on exhalation. Feel your hands upon your thighs. Notice any tension in the body, and try to release it while still maintaining good posture. Remember your breath, and return your focus to your breath. Breathe, in and out, giving your breath your entire attention.

If you feel an ache in your back or shoulders that's fine, let it be. Your back is not used to holding itself in good posture, and the muscles will develop over time. Simply relax, keeping the spine erect. Send love to any aches or pains in your body, radiating love outwards from your heart. Breathe into any tension, and let it go with each exhale. Then, bring your attention back to your breath.

Keep the eyes soft, unfocused. Let them relax, wide awake and aware. Let your body relax, wide awake and aware. Feel the air on your skin, the space around your body. Feel the cushion and floor beneath you. Feel your body as it sits in stillness in the meditative position. Breath in, and out, in and out.

Listen to the sounds around you. Listen, without judgement. Name the sounds in your mind, and then let them go. Be aware of all that is happening around you, and then return to your breath. In, out. In, out.

If thoughts enter your mind, notice them, name them and let them go, focusing once again on the breath, in, out. In, out. Do not get wrapped up in thoughts, just notice and let go. Feel your body, stable and still. Return to your breath, in, and out.

Be aware of your body, of the space that you are in. Be aware of your breath. Be in the present moment, without judgement. Enjoy the stillness, the silence.

You can extend this basic mindfulness meditation to any length of time that you wish. You may desire to begin with the basic meditation, and perhaps then move onto prayer, or even begin with prayer and end with basic meditation. You may like to end the meditation with a blessing, such as:

Blessed be the precious and preserving air,
The breath of life, our inspiration and delight.
Blessed be the precious and preserving fire,
The blood of life, our warming guest.
Blessed be the precious and preserving water,
The water of life, our cleansing guest.
Blessed be the precious and preserving earth,
The flesh of life, our sustainer and our wisdom.
– Caitlin Matthews, from *Celtic Devotional: Daily Prayers and Blessings*

You may wish to incorporate *mudras,* hand positions in your meditation that are like yoga for the hands, uniting your body with a different spiritual and/or corporeal energy. Popular mudras are the Cosmic Mudra, Namaste Mudra and the Om Mudra. You can also simply switch from palms down on your thighs, (which helps to ground and centre) to palms up (which keeps you open to the energies around you).

Cosmic Mudra: This is done by placing your dominant hand faced palm up in your lap, cupping your other hand also faced palm up. The thumbs are lightly touching.

Namaste Mudra: Perform this by pressing the palms together (a traditional prayer position in many faiths), with fingertips pointing up and the thumbs gently resting at the sternum, the heart centre. This mudra has the same meaning as the Sanskrit greeting *Namaste*, which is accompanied by a slight bowing of the head, as a gesture of honouring the divinity in both the self and others.

Om Mudra: In each hand, bring the index finger and the thumb together so that the tips are touching, and rest each hand on the knees or thighs. Om Mudra represents the union of divine energy and the self.

If you are familiar with journeying meditations, you can use the basic mindfulness meditation to begin and end these sessions. What matters most is that the basic meditation is done at least once a day, to enable you to find some space and silence in order to quiet the mind and find integration in the present moment. Begin small, if you have not meditated before, and work your way up to 30 minutes or more.

Rooted in the present moment, we can carry the meditative and peaceful feeling with us throughout the day and night, as we are truly awake and aware to the natural world.

Part Four – Mindfulness

Mindfulness is THE buzzword in self-improvement and New Age circles, and now in healthcare; but what does it really mean? If we go back to basics, we find that it is rooted in Zen Buddhism, and can be easily explained in two simple phrases.

Chop wood. Carry water.

This is actually a pared down version of a slightly longer Zen story, wherein an enlightened monk recalls his process to enlightenment. He stated: 'When I was unenlightened, I chopped wood and carried water. When I became enlightened, I chopped wood and carried water.'

A lot of the time it can feel like we're carrying wood and chopping water: burdened and not really getting anywhere, flailing around with a dripping axe. But when we stop, focus and concentrate, usually things become smoother, get done quicker and with little drama. Some may not want that; they enjoy the distraction that the flailing causes, the drama. After a while though, it can wear thin. Applying mindfulness, which is simply paying attention, can help alleviate any dis-ease or suffering that we may feel in our lives. That's not to say that we'll feel great all the time, however, just by being in the present moment and not attaching to past experiences, dwelling on them or getting stuck in an emotion we can just get on with plain *living*.

Mindfulness is bringing the concept of non-attachment to everything that we do, utterly living in the present moment. We will still feel and have emotions, but we will be able to let them go in order to see the present moment for what it is, unclouded by our attachment to the past, anxieties about the future, our egos and more. We will be able to respond to situations with more grace, compassion and be more at peace with the world. We will ease our suffering and the suffering of others if we are aware of all the attachment that comes with modern living. We will find interconnectedness and great reverence for all existence.

Chapter Sixteen

Mindful Mondays and the Present Moment

Why not dedicate an entire day to mindfulness each week? Ideally, we try to be mindful all the time, but we're not perfect. Having an entire day to focus on mindfulness will hopefully trickle down into everything we do in the rest of the week: all our thoughts, actions and their consequences. I've deemed this my Mindful Mondays in my own practice.

So, what does this all mean? It means that when we're eating breakfast, we're just eating breakfast, not reading a book or article. When we're washing the dishes, we're just washing the dishes and not singing along to the our favourite album. When we're out walking, we are walking mindfully, at whatever speed, paying attention to our steps and our surroundings, not planning our evening meal. When we're stroking the cat, we're not thinking about writing the next chapter of our book. When we're driving we're really feeling the road beneath us, not dwelling on the driver who decided to overtake us on a blind summit. When we're out for a meal with friends, we're really paying attention to what they are saying, and not already forming a reply to their words before they've even finished talking.

Mindful Mondays are all about paying attention.

With centred awareness, with that focus, we can simplify our lives immensely. People often fear that we will be less productive, because we seem to be doing less, but actually we will do jobs better, more efficiently, if we maintain that focus.

Mindfulness of the body is a great gift you can give to yourself. Being aware of your movements is doing a great kindness to your body. When we are walking down the stairs, we are focusing on our body moving. We will find that our movements may become less hurried and more graceful. Calm descends on our way of being. We have fewer accidents, and fewer resulting lumps and bumps. Like a leaf falling from the tree, we simply are in that moment, moving as the wind suggests, awake to every moment.

So, like the monk who realised that life doesn't change after enlightenment and that you still have to do the things you have to do, what you can change is *how* you do them: mindfully, with awareness, focus and concentration. Even if a day is too much, try an hour or half an hour each day. Eat a meal in mindfulness. Clean the bathroom in mindfulness. Play with the children in mindfulness. You don't have to change your schedule, just do everything in it mindfully.

The present moment

Being comfortable in the present moment is key to finding lasting happiness. Awareness of the past serves only as a guide to the present moment, helping us to release many things that can have a negative effect on the present moment such as anger, grief, fear or hate. Knowing that the future is only a flexible plan helps us to not get too stuck in our ways and habits, and can also alleviate feelings such as fear. Our focus should always been on the here and now, living life fully.

But what if the 'now' isn't all that great? What if in the 'now' we are stuck outside in the pouring rain without an umbrella or coat, waiting for a bus that never turns up? Yes, that's all part of it. Buddhism teaches in the first noble truth that all beings suffer. You can't escape it. That might sound pretty pessimistic, but the upside is that the other noble truths help us to alleviate that suffering. One of the ways to do so is to fully be in your self, in your body and mind (there is no separation) and in doing so the suffering eases. That doesn't mean you won't get soaked to your underwear, but instead you spent the time feeling the rain upon your body, smelling the earth responding to the rain and smiling to your own heart rather than becoming angry at the bus driver, becoming grumpy about the wetness, or wondering why this sort of thing always happens to you.

For some people who are living in extreme conditions, in the middle of a war zone for instance, the above may sound trite. However, Vietnamese monk Thich Nhat Hanh experienced the horrors of war first hand and learned how to be in the present moment, to help alleviate the suffering. (See *The Miracle of Mindfulness* by Thich Nhat Hanh.) When we are in the present moment we will know how to respond to any situation better than if we are responding from the past or future. Our clarity sharpens and we respond in a manner that is wholly and utterly relevant to the situation at hand rather than dredging up issues from the past or worries about the future.

We all have had to deal with uncomfortable situations and difficult people. Being in the present helps us to not dredge up the past and project it onto a particular situation in negative ways, rather it enables us to deal with the issues as they are, up front without any extra baggage. That doesn't necessarily mean that we enjoy dealing with this sort of stuff, but we can get through it with a lighter heart, finding our peace more quickly and being able to spread that out to the world. It helps us to see reality, as it really is. Eventually you may find that your inner peace becomes less and less disturbed, no matter what life throws at you, and that peace and calm will radiate out into the world in beautiful and positive ways.

Remember the old saying, 'Yesterday's the past, tomorrow's the future, but today is a gift. That's why it's called the present.'

Things to do and try:

- Try a Mindful Monday, or spend a half-day, a couple of hours, in total mindfulness. You can begin with even smaller tasks, and build up to a half-day, then a full day of mindfulness. Wash the dishes in mindfulness. Fold the laundry in mindfulness. Ride the bus in mindfulness.

- Find things around you that can help you to remember mindfulness. Look at the sky to remind you of the beauty around you. When you hear the chime of a clock, stop and breathe, being utterly aware and present in the moment.

Chapter Seventeen

Animism and the Present Moment

For many people, myself included, Druidry and Animism go hand in hand. Since the coming of Christianity and also the Age of Enlightenment, Animism has gotten the reputation of being somehow backward, a superstitious and childish view of the world wherein everything is 'alive'. This belief is completely biased in that it is totally from a human-centric point of view; those who believe it to be silly would say that believing a stone has a soul is absolutely ridiculous. This point of view is a projection of our human perspective, of what is alive and what isn't, what is ensouled and what is not. It doesn't take into consideration differences in the metaphysical. This perspective is often derogatory of Animism, yet it fails to actually understand just what Animism actually means, and what living with an Animistic perspective can bring to human consciousness and awareness.

In my opinion, we are in great debt to author Emma Restall Orr for exploring Animism in her two books, *Living With Honour* and *The Wakeful World*. In both she describes just what it means to be an Animist, putting aside the childish perspective and engaging with the concept in a very rational and yet spiritual manner. In these two books, she shows the interconnectedness of all things in contexts of philosophy, spirituality and science.

This interconnectedness is reflected in many, if not most, religions and spiritualities throughout the world. Zen monk Thich Nhat Hanh uses the term 'interbeing', founding *The Order of Interbeing* as a way to live your life fully aware of the interconnectedness of all things. We cannot exist without each other; we are fully co-existing together. In a piece of paper, there is the sun, the tree, the rain, the wind, nitrogen, carbon dioxide, stars, clouds, loggers, factory workers, their ancestors, the ancestors of place, the foods that they ate; the list goes on forever. Since the beginning of time, if there ever was a beginning, we all came from the same source, if there is a single source. We are all star-stuff. We are awake and aware to it. We are mindful of all that exists in the present moment.

This interconnectedness is fascinating, and can help guide us in our Zen Druid path every step of the way. Every decision we make is based upon our interconnectedness, from what we have for breakfast to how we talk to people, the mileage in the use of our cars and the rituals that we participate in. When we honour all life within us and in the world, we can truly see that there can be no separation, only integration. The wound in modern society created by our separation from the natural world is only illusion, for we can never be separate. It is harder to see when living in urban environments, for example, because the thread of humanity can be so overpowering, or living in a war torn country, where violence deafens the natural order and harmony. Only by grasping this concept and moving beyond it, taking it into practise, can we begin to understand the nature of existence, and indeed, the meaning of life.

Working with concepts of Animism, we walk through our lives with more awareness, and perhaps even more grace. We see ourselves within the ebola virus, in the cancer cell. We see these things are part of our selves. The cancer cell is just as much a part of my body as is any other cell. This does not mean that if I have cancer cells in my body I should just submit, and die of cancer. If I contract the ebola virus, I shouldn't just submit to it, allowing it to live and take over, dying as a result. Animism and Druidry is not about submission. If I submit to the river or the sea, I drown. If I submit to anger, my life becomes anger. If I submit to the elements, I will die of exposure. Mindfulness, not submission, is key here in all that we do.

Many people often mistake humility for humiliation. Humility is seeing that we are not better than anything else;

humiliation is where something makes us less than we are. There is a distinct difference between the two. Being mindful and humble is a good way to live, as it allows us to truly see the interconnectedness of all things without our egos getting in the way. Allowing others to humiliate us goes a step outside of that, creating separation, and allowing submission.

Mindfulness in the present moment, awake and aware to all life, seeing all life in every aspect of being: this is at the heart of Animism and also Zen.

The beauty and wonder of the present moment are there for us all to enjoy. All we have to do is open our perception to see them. In the midst of great suffering there is the possibility of great compassion. In this compassion there is the power of love and beauty, two words that may be bandied about recklessly in our modern-day society, but these words, concepts and energies have real power within them.

Through our suffering, we can make small steps towards awareness and mindfulness by becoming awake and attentive, thereby easing our suffering and that of the world around us. We notice things that we wouldn't otherwise notice in our suffering, as we turn our gaze outwards and perceive the world in its entirety rather than just our own suffering. Thich Nhat Hanh is a wonderful example of one who has seen and experienced the suffering of war, of exile, of persecution and physical trauma and still sees the power of love and beauty in the world around him. *'When I suffer, I shall breathe in and out, look at the sky, the trees, into the eyes of a loved one and know happiness and joy, there finding the deepest gratitude for my blessings.'*

Things to help create a mindful presence:

- Explore Animism, and become aware of the interconnectedness of all things.
- Practice meditation each and every day, to increase your ability for mindfulness.

Part Five – Integration

As Druids we seek a deep relationship with the world around us. This relationship causes us to integrate into our environment, understanding that we are a part of a whole and not separate from the rest of existence. To that end, we become a fully functioning, contributing part of the whole. When we live a life in service to the whole, then we learn the value of relationship, becoming a seamless part of the bigger picture.

Chapter Eighteen

Ego, the Self and Identity

The self is our truth, our essence, the energy that combines with form to give rise to the being known as you in this current manifestation. We understand that manifestation is undergoing perpetual change. We are born, grow, mature and die. We return to the soil to become a new manifestation of life, in the tree planted on our grave, inside the creepy-crawlies and bacteria that will feed upon our flesh, in the moisture of the soil that will evaporate, turning us into clouds and rain and so on. We are energy, every single one of us, and we understand that energy cannot be destroyed. Energy can only change in its manifestation.

The ego is the story that we tell our self about our self. It is a construct that keeps us defined within the limits of the story that we keep. It creates boundaries between *Us* and *Them*. Knowing as we do that we cannot exist separately, that we need the existence of many other life forms, we know that in our co-dependent arising or manifestation that we are not alone. The ego is an illusion to keep us feeling separated, usually in order to preserve its own existence. We have learned that everyone has a Buddha nature, that we are all part of ecosystems within ecosystems, and that no one part is more important than the other. As Zen Druids, we know that we have to be vigilant when it comes to our egos, in order to ensure that we are not living within them, but rather aware of them and working instead towards complete integration.

The ego, however, is not always a bad thing. If we consider that we have two parts to our ego, the functional ego and the representational ego, then we can work more positively towards integration without losing our sense of identity. I sometimes refer to these as functional and representational 'self' in other work, but here we will attribute them to ego in order to better understand the ego in relation to identity and the self.

The functional ego helps us to perceive the world through our senses. It is a clear lens that we can use to look at any given situation, unsullied by things like judgement or partisan points of view. It makes choices based on the reality of the present moment. Combined with mindful awareness it creates a holistic and harmonious way of living. The functional ego helps us to get on with our everyday life, in the manifestation known as yourself, without anything like self-aggrandisement, or poor self-esteem getting in the way.

The representational ego is the story that we tell ourselves, but through the distorted lens of past experience, judgement and even anxiety about the future. The representational ego seeks to distract us from the reality of the present moment by placing judgements, rigid opinions, self-centred thoughts and even deceptions, self-deceptions and outright lies in order to preserve its delicate state and to make us feel better about ourselves. When we see through the representational ego's *modus operandi*, we are able to make better decisions in our life that are not all about trying to preserve our egos, but about really trying to make the world a better place, living in harmony with it in everything that we do.

Representational ego creates boundaries that bring about the illusion of separation. It confines us within certain limitations in order to preserve its own existence. We may not even be aware of the boundaries or separation that it creates, so ingrained are they in our culture. The limitations can extend to race, nationality, gender, species, job descriptions and more. Functional ego doesn't limit self to these boundaries, but transcends them. We begin to understand that the whole universe is contained within our form, and vice versa. The Song of Amergin is a brilliant Druid perspective of the functional ego, not limiting itself in any shape or form, but seeing its manifestation in all shapes and form.

I am the wind on the sea
I am the wave of the sea
I am the bull of seven battles
I am the eagle on the rock
I am a flash from the sun
I am the most beautiful of plants
I am a strong wild boar
I am a salmon in the water
I am a lake in the plain
I am the word of knowledge
I am the head of the spear in battle
I am the God that puts fire in the head
Who spreads light in the gathering on the hills?
Who can tell the ages of the moon?
Who can tell the place where the sun rests?
– Translation by Lady Augusta Gregory, from *Gods and Fighting Men: The Story of the Tuatha De Danaan and of the Fianna of Ireland*

We see here the integration that is at the heart of Druidry, as well as the lessening of the sense of a separate self that is at the heart of Zen.

Representational ego creates a subject/object divide. It is unable to perceive something without seeing it through the lens of the ego and attachment. The attachment of the ego is at the heart of much suffering in the world. Working from a place of constant defensiveness, the perception created is distorted and we find ourselves constantly reacting instead of acting with clear intention. We may take slight at the smallest thing, because we are so attached to our self-created self, instead of seeing that we are all related. Someone might criticise or say something that you don't agree with, and suddenly the representational ego sees this as a threat to its own existence. It then works to destroy whatever or whomever contradicts or criticises its story in any shape or form, often without thought. When we are able to use the clear lens of perception through the functional ego, we aren't so defensive; we aren't living in a state of threat or reaction to the threat. We are able to smile, see the little demons that try to cause division, and remind ourselves that we are all made of star-stuff. When we see the bigger picture, we find out what is truly important, and stop wasting our time on all the small stuff.

Western dualism is so ingrained in our society that it becomes very difficult to change our perception to the clear lens of functional ego. We have to truly understand that mind and body are not two separate things, even as we understand that we are all related. It is the impermanence of all things that is so central to the Zen way of life that inspires us on our path towards integration. Our society fuels the ego like no other. Social media is a great place where one can either be puffed up or dragged down by people one has never met. People can use social media to help fuel the ego, and not in altogether productive ways. Expressing your creativity is a great way to give back to the world. Why not put up that piece of artwork that you've worked so hard on? Give us an excerpt from your latest book. Tell us of the charity work that you are doing in India. This is an expression of yourself that is not separated from your functional self. It's not all representational, unless you are totally attached to it.

Why are we so addicted to our story, to our self-centred perception? The representational ego is constantly devoting all its energy to reinforcing itself, and can do so through creating drama, attention-seeking or distraction from suffering just to name a few. We begin to live inside our heads, inside our stories and do not seek alternative points of view. We can become deluded by our story, confirmed by people we may have never even met. We can react viciously to things that upset us, through online comments, blog posts, etc. We take it from the virtual world into the real world. Why would we want to do this? Why would we want to hurt another? Why should this be? Is it because the ego is such a fragile thing? Yes, indeed. Yet it is important to remember that this illusion is just an illusion.

The representational ego seeks to reaffirm itself in everything that it does. It's based on its own self-preservation, fuelled by an erroneous concept that one would lose their identity with the loss of ego. This couldn't be further from the truth. There are plenty of people out there with a very strong sense of identity and purpose, yet who are not fuelled by their representational ego. These people are inspiring, for they know that the work they do and how they live their life is more important that *who* they are.

No one is perfect. Everyone succumbs to their representational ego every now and then. But when we live entirely through this ego's whimsy, then we are in big trouble. We may see other people's success as our failure. We may take slight at something because we haven't been included in it. We might want to make someone look bad and undermine everything that they do because they have hurt us in some shape or form. We cease to see with the eyes of compassion, instead only seeing through the eyes of 'ME'.

Where does this all lead? Is it worth it? What will be the outcome of living in this ego?

It will not be happiness. We will rage against those who argue against us. We will delude ourselves with notions of grandeur, or delusions of all shapes and forms. We will spend an inordinate amount of time thinking about things that don't really matter. We will spend all our time reinforcing the ego. What really matters in life: the ego, or living well?

Mindfulness and meditation are the medicine for this dis-ease, helping us to see beyond the illusion. We find that we have no need, no craving, no attachment to our story. We recognise our own history, but we see it clearly, unclouded by judgement and attachment. Stories flow and change. The ancient Druids had an oral tradition, which recognised the dangers of committing ideas to the static perceptions we see in our world today. In mindfulness we bring our soul back to its true form. We break free of the limitations that we have place upon ourselves, those fence posts that we believe keep us safe and secure when really they only hold us back. We have a strong sense of identity, of who we are, guided by our ancestors of the past, present and future. We know who we are, but we are not attached to it, knowing that we are also much, much more. We do the work, we know what is important in life. We run out into the wilds with open hearts and open minds, able to truly experience life to its fullest.

Things to consider:

- What is the story of yourself that you have told people?
- What is the story of yourself that has been told to you by others?
- How much does this story reflect who you really are?
- How is daily meditation changing your perspective?
- Meditate upon the notion of 'saving face'. When have you had to do so in your life? Consider thoughts and actions of saving face, and whether they were really worth it. How much time and energy was spent in the endeavour? Could you have spent this time more wisely?
- Do not judge yourself too harshly for having done things out of representational ego. Instead, be compassionate with yourself and focus on what's important, right here, right now. Live well.

Chapter Nineteen

Awen and Relationship

The Celts are believed to have had Indo-European roots, migrating across Europe and leaving their mark across many countries. They share many similar spiritual beliefs with other traditions: Buddhist, Saxon and Norse just to name a few. There are similarities in artwork and other modes of creative expression. Finding something that is 'pure' in any tradition is, at least in my opinion, unattainable. We are constantly being influenced by other people, whether it was 50, 500 or 5,000 years ago.

Zen and Druidry blend together to form a life path that is utterly devoted to being in the present moment, giving the Druid total immersion within nature. This immersion, not just going with the flow but being the flow itself, is what makes it so special. Zen teaches us to let go of our sense of self, to silence our chattering minds in order to be able to pay attention to the world at large. It also teaches us discipline, learning how our minds work and how we are frequently ruled by our emotions, bad habits, reactionary living, destructive behaviour and so on.

With zazen, or sitting meditation, the mind is brought under control through hours and hours of practise, of learning to simply 'be', slowly and gently silencing our mind, enabling us to hear the songs of the universe. It is allowing other songs, other voices to be heard above our own so that we may better integrate. We will still have opinions, but we will cherish them less, for we know that everything is in constant flux. We will have a sense of self, but again we hold to it lightly so that we may better see where we fit in the world and where we can do the most good. It is not annihilation. It is immersion, awareness and mindfulness.

Within Druidry, we learn to work with awen, with inspiration and the flow of life to see where we fit in the grand scheme of things. We work to see how we can live with the least harm to ourselves and the planet, and also what we can do to make the world a better place. We are inspired by our relationships and we inspire others in return. We work to create peace within ourselves and peace in the outer world as well. Using our natural abilities and skills, we may work with songs and poetry, or with visions or herbal medicine, with roles in teaching and counselling, in law or in environmentalism; the list is endless. We are devoted to helping and conserving nature and our planet, sharing the awen, the inspiration, and giving back with gratitude for what we have received.

Using the techniques from Zen for training the mind and the love of nature from Druidry we can find a way to immerse ourselves in our spirituality that is deeply integrated on so many levels. When out walking in the forest, we can lose our sense of self in order to become the forest. Once we are the forest, we are able to drink deeply from the flow of awen that is all around us. We become the trees, the deer, the fox, the boulder, the streams and the badger. We can learn so much from this integration that can also rejuvenate us, providing us with even more inspiration. We are not looking at ourselves being at one in the forest; we have lost even that in order to become the forest. When we are fully immersed in simply 'being', we are fully in the flow of awen, of relationship. We *are* the forest.

Our footsteps become lighter, our passage barely noticeable. Like the deer, we are able to bound through the trees, awake and aware to every sense. Indeed, all our senses become sharper, clearer, for our minds are not running us ragged thinking about what to have for dinner, the paper that is due, the meeting we have on Monday. Fully in the moment, we become the awen, the connecting thread where soul touches soul, where integration, understanding, inspiration and compassion occur.

Zen Buddhism contributes the idea of compassion. Again, many people misinterpret compassion, seeing it as weak, or being a pushover. Why be kind to others when so few are kind to us? Living with compassion is what enables us to connect once again to that all-important word in Druidry – awen. The songs of life can only be heard if we try to understand them. We cannot understand them unless we open ourselves to compassion.

Awen and peace – East meets West

Further exploring the nature of peace, what leads us to understand the fundamental precept behind achieving peace is compassion. But what is compassion?

Dictionary definitions say that it is a state of sympathy with someone who is suffering, and yet that doesn't adequately describe compassion in my mind, in either the Zen or the Druid tradition. Two words in Sanskrit delve a little closer, such as *karuna*, a gentle affection and a willingness to bear others' pain, or *metta*, often described now as *loving kindness*, acting for the benefit of all living things with a selfless attitude.

The Dalai Lama stated:

Genuine compassion must have both wisdom and loving kindness. That is to say, one must understand the nature of the suffering from which we wish to free others (this is wisdom), and one must experience deep intimacy and empathy with other sentient beings (this is loving kindness).
– The Essence of the Heart Sutra

Compassion is all about relationship, about integration with the world, with the universe. As the Lakota Native American saying goes: 'We are all related.' In order for this integration to occur, we have to learn how to lose our sense of self, for if there is a separate self, there can be no true integration, only the state of sympathy. There is someone observing someone else's suffering, and helping to alleviate their suffering but still retaining a sense of Us and Them. In Buddhism, wisdom, or *prajna*, is most often found through the teachings of *No Self*, or *attana*.

In Zen Buddhism, we are taught to help wherever we can, as selflessly as is possible (No Self), which is true compassion. If you help someone and then expect a reward, there is still a separate self expecting a reward from a separate person. We have to learn to drop all expectations. The Tibetan practice of *Lojong* ends with a final slogan that is brilliant in this regard: *Do Not Expect Applause*. Only then is there is there an integration of everyone involved, with no subject/object duality.

In Druidry, this integration is often called relationship, but again, words fail to describe the enormity of the meaning behind it all. Druidry also uses the word *awen*, a Welsh word with several interpretations: poetic inspiration and flowing spirit to name a few. Awen is relationship and integration, the connecting threads that bind us, soul to soul.

To find true peace, one must release into this, into awen, losing that sense of separateness, and in doing so discovering the nature of compassion in soul to soul relationship.

Relationship

Druidry is all about relationship, and you cannot have relationship without some form of communication. It may not always be in words, human to human, but opening the lines of communication helps us to perceive that the world is more than just our own sense of self. When we begin to see that there are other perspectives, other points of view, we also come to an awareness that the world is being experienced by each being individually, in a collective state of unity or reality dictated by space and time.

Year after year events around the world shine a spotlight on discordance, in human to human relationship, and in human to other-than-human relationships. Violent attacks, disregard for the environment, the increasing gap between the rich and the poor and more can be attributed to an 'Us' and 'Them' mentality.

When we remove this dualist point of view and encompass a more holistic approach, we see that what we do to others, we do to ourselves. In Zen Buddhism, it is acknowledged that suffering exists in the world, and that this suffering is caused by the illusion of separation. If we look deeply enough scientifically, anthropologically, and even spiritually we can see that there is more that binds us together than tears us apart.

As a Druid, nature teaches us the impermanence of all things, through the cycles of birth, death and energy in constant motion. It teaches us of unity and ancestry, for in our bodies are electrons that have previously been in trees, in a child in Mexico, in the deer and in the blackbird. The air that we breathe is the breath of the ancestors, and the shared breath of the world. We all have star-stuff within us. Not in a 'hippy-dippy' sense, but in a real, visceral sense that this connection is all pervasive; we simply choose to ignore it for whatever reason.

Nature also teaches us of circumstance, for certain seeds will grow differently in various soils. Our lives are mostly comfortable here in the West, and afford us the opportunity for quiet reflection. We are not being shot at, or suffering from hunger for the most part. Nature teaches us of circumstances, which in turn provides us with a lesson in humility. This lesson reinforces the perspective that one person is not better or worse than another, but is simply living under different conditions. Compassion is a great teacher, based in a wider perspective where circumstance and environment have a huge part to play in how we judge and take stock of our lives and the world.

Nature also teaches us of the way to work together to create harmonious union in an environment, to work for the benefit of the whole, in symbiosis, to be a part of a functioning ecosystem without messing it all up. It teaches us that hatred towards any being has no place in our lives, though we may hate the suffering that chains people in their situations. We know that we can work towards ending that suffering, as Druids, as peacemakers, as human beings. If we sow the seeds of love and compassion, respect and integrity we can have a hope for the future. That doesn't mean that the storms will pass us by, or that we will not suffer, but we can weather the storms through our relationship with the gods, the land and the ancestors, and hopefully lead by example without setting ourselves up as some sort of martyr.

Perhaps it is more about finding your place in the world, your place in your environment that gives your life meaning, even as your sense of self falls away in beautiful integration. In this, relationship is the key, for we have to open the lines of communication in order to understand more than our own point of view.

Everything is interconnected; we simply could not exist were it not for the countless forms of other life on this planet. In scientific understanding, all life came from single-celled organisms that evolved into life as we know it. We all, everything on this planet, have a common ancestor.

Yet we are constantly bombarded by the dualistic thinking that has plagued our species for many, many years. We often feel separated from nature, from the world, from other human beings, from our ancestors. It is often reinforced through marketing, various theologies and psychology, in most cases to ensure that there is repeat business, power and normalisation.

We are, however, all connected, and it is through personal relationships with place that the Zen Druid creates their worldview, learning from the land upon which they live, the ancestors and the gods. This is awen, soul to soul relationship. In Animism, we realise that there is no such thing as a 'thing'; we cannot look at anything (pardon the pun) in this regard. When we use the term 'thing' we can often objectify it, not giving it the inherent right to existence that Animism honours. Many native traditions use the term 'brother', 'sister', 'grandmother' or 'grandfather' when speaking of a life form that is non-human, whether it be a non-human animal, the moon, the sea, a tree, the sky. In that way, relationship is acknowledged and inherent respect is created. A community is created, an ecosystem in every sense of the word. We are all descended from a few ancestors. We are all family. We have the stuff of stars in our blood and in our bodies, minerals found in distant galaxies. The flow of awen, the soul to soul relationship, blossoms and inspires.

As Zen Druids, we have to remember this in everything that we do. We have to ensure that we are not falling into the traps of dualism, marketing, secular culture and more. We have to see the beauty and awe in everything, and live a life that is filled with awareness of what threads connect us to the world. These threads will then shimmer with profound awen, where soul touches soul in true relationship, sacred relationship.

Things to think about:

- Awen is often termed as inspiration: What inspires you? How can that inspiration lead to a deeper relationship with the world? Follow those flows of energy and see how life changes as a result.
- Meditate upon your ancestry, both human and non-human. Trace the threads back through time in your mind, and come to an awareness of true relationship.
- Awen is not only about receiving inspiration, but breathing that back into the world. Use your creativity and ingenuity to give back for the inspiration that you have received. Use your talent, your gifts, your abilities to their truest potential.

Final Words...

I hope that this book has helped you to deepen your studies in both Zen and Druidry, to help create a life path that is wholly awake and aware of the beauty of the present moment, integrated within the world in soul-deep relationship. The creation of this book and my previous work, *Zen Druidry*, is based on my experience with the two traditions and the result of fifteen years' personal experience combining Eastern and Western traditions. It is my firm belief that there is no monopoly on wisdom, and we should learn all we can from this life we are gifted, in whatever capacity we are able. May your journey be blessed.

Bibliography and Suggested Reading

Adamson, E. & McClain, G. (2001) *The Complete Idiot's Guide to Zen Living*: Alpha

Allen, R. (2002) *Zen Questions:* London: MQ Publications Limited

Beck, C.J. (1997) *Everyday Zen:* London: Thorsons

Beck, C.J. (1995) *Nothing Special: Living Zen* New York: Harper Collins

Carr-Gomm, P. (2002) *Druid Mysteries: Ancient Wisdom for the 21st Century*: Rider

Gregory, A. (2014) *Gods and Fighting Men: The Story of the Tuatha De Danaan and of the Fianna of Ireland*: CreateSpace Independent Publishing Platform

Hanh, T.N. (2001) *Anger: Buddhist Wisdom for Cooling the Flames*: Rider

Hanh, T.N. (2012) *Making Space: Creating a Home Meditation Practice*: Parallax Press

Hanh, T.N. (2015) *No Mud, No Lotus: The Art of Transforming Suffering*: Parallax Press

Hanh, T.N. (2008) *The Miracle of Mindfulness*: Rider, Classic Ed Edition

Hanh, T.N. (1993) *Interbeing: Fourteen Guidelines for Engaged Buddhism*: Parallax Press

Hutton, R. (2011) *Blood and Mistletoe: The History of the Druids in Britain*: Yale University Press

Kirkey, J. (2009) *The Salmon in the Spring: The Ecology of Celtic Spirituality*: Hiraeth Press

Lama, D. (2005) *Essence of the Heart Sutra: The Dalai Lama's Heart of Wisdom Teachings*: Wisdom Publications, U.S.

MacEowan, F.H. (2002) *The Mist-filled Path: Celtic Wisdom for Exiles, Wanderers and Seekers*: New World Library

Matthews, C. (2004) *Celtic Devotional: Daily Prayers and Blessings*: Gill & Macmillan Ltd

Talboys, G. (2002) *Way of the Druid: Rebirth of an Ancient Religion*: O-Books

Tzu, L. (2002) *The Complete Works of Lao Tzu: Translation and Elucidation by Hua-Ching Ni*: Sevenstar Communications U.S.

Restall Orr, E. (2004) *Living Druidry: Magical Spirituality for the Wild Sou:* London: Piatkus Books Ltd

Restall Orr, E. (2007) *Living With Honour: A Pagan Ethics:* O-Books

Restall Orr, E. (2000) *Ritual: A Guide to Life, Love & Inspiration* London: Thorsons

Restall Orr, E. (2012) *The Wakeful World: Animism, Mind and the Self in Nature*: Moon Books

van der Hoeven, J. (2014) *The Awen Alone: Walking the Path of the Solitary Druid*: Moon Books

van der Hoeven, J. (2013) *Zen Druidry: Living a Natural Life in Full Awareness*: Moon Books

Internet Resources

Order of Interbeing www.orderofinterbeing.org
The British Druid Order www.druidry.co.uk
The Druid Network www.druidnetwork.org
The Order of Bards, Ovates and Druids www.druidry.org
Zen Buddhism www.sacred-texts.com/bud/zen/index.htm
Zen Guide www.zenguide.com

Other Books by the Author

Zen Druidry: Living a Natural Life with Full Awareness
Taking both Zen and Druidry and integrating them into your life can be a wonderful and ongoing process of discovery, not only of the self but also of the entire world around you. Looking at ourselves and at the natural world around us, we realise that everything is in constant flux: like waves on the ocean, they are all united as a body of water. Even after the wave crashes upon the shore, the ocean is still there, the wave is still there; it has merely changed its form. The aim of this text is an introduction to how Zen teachings and Druidry can combine, creating a peaceful life path that is completely and utterly dedicated to the here and now, to the earth and her rhythms, and to the flow that is life itself.

The Awen Alone: Walking the Path of the Solitary Druid
Druidry is a wonderful, spiritually fulfilling life path. Through the magic of Druidry, we build deep and abiding relationships with the natural world around us, and through our connection to the natural environment we walk a path of truth, honour and service. Throughout the ages, people have withdrawn from the world in order to connect more fully with it. This book is an introductory guide for those who wish to walk the Druid path alone, for however long a time. It is about exploration and connection with the natural world, and finding our place within it. It covers the basics of Druidry and how, when applied to everyday life, enriches it with a sense of beauty, magic and mystery. This book is for those who feel called to seek their own path, to use their wit and intelligence, compassion and honour to create their own tradition within Druidry.

Dancing With Nemetona: A Druid's Exploration of Sanctuary and Sacred Space

Nemetona is an ancient goddess whose song is heard deep within the earth and also deep within the human soul. She is the Lady of Sanctuary, of Sacred Groves and Sacred Spaces. She is present within the home, within our sacred groves, our rites and in all the spaces that we hold dear to our hearts. She also lies within, allowing us to feel at ease wherever we are in the world through her energy of holding and of transformation. She is the energy of sacred space, where we can stretch out our souls and truly come alive, filled with the magic of potential. Rediscover this ancient goddess and dance with a Druid to the songs of Nemetona. Learn how to reconnect with this goddess in ritual, songs, chants, meditation and more.

About the Author

Joanna van der Hoeven was born in Quebec, Canada. She moved to the UK in 1998, where she now lives with her husband in a small village in Suffolk, near the coast of the North Sea.

Joanna is a Druid, author, teacher, poet, singer and dancer. She has studied with Emma Restall Orr and the Order of Bards, Ovates and Druids. She has a BA Hons English Language and Literature degree. She is currently the media co-ordinator for The Druid Network also works as a Druid priestess for her community. She is also co-founder and tutor at Druid College UK. She gives talks and workshops regularly on meditation, Druidry, Zen Buddhism and more.

For more information, please visit
www.joannavanderhoeven.com

Moon Books invites you to begin or deepen your encounter with
Paganism, in all its rich, creative, flourishing forms.

If you have enjoyed this book, why not tell other readers by posting a review on your preferred booksite. Recent bestsellers from Moon Books are:

Journey to the Dark Goddess
How to Return to Your Soul
Jane Meredith
Discover the powerful secrets of the Dark Goddess and transform your depression, grief and pain into healing and integration.
Paperback: 978-1-84694-677-6
ebook: 978-1-78099-223-5

Shamanic Reiki
Expanded Ways of Working with Universal Life Force Energy
Llyn Roberts, Robert Levy
Shamanism and Reiki are each powerful ways of healing; together, their power multiplies. *Shamanic Reiki* introduces techniques to help healers and Reiki practitioners tap ancient healing wisdom.
Paperback: 978-1-84694-037-8
ebook: 978-1-84694-650-9

Pagan Portals – The Awen Alone
Walking the Path of the Solitary Druid
Joanna van der Hoeven
An introductory guide for the solitary Druid, *The Awen Alone* will accompany you as you explore and seek out your own place within the natural world.
Paperback: 978-1-78279-547-6
ebook: 978-1-78279-546-9

A Kitchen Witch's World of Magical Herbs & Plants

Rachel Patterson

A journey into the magical world of herbs and plants, filled with magical uses, folklore, history and practical magic. By popular writer, blogger and kitchen witch, Tansy Firedragon.

Paperback: 978-1-78279-621-3

ebook: 978-1-78279-620-6

Medicine for the Soul

The Complete Book of Shamanic Healing

Ross Heaven

All you will ever need to know about shamanic healing and how to become your own shaman...

Paperback: 978-1-78099-419-2

ebook: 978-1-78099-420-8

Shaman Pathways – The Druid Shaman

Exploring the Celtic Otherworld

Danu Forest

A practical guide to Celtic shamanism with exercises and techniques as well as traditional lore for exploring the Celtic Otherworld.

Paperback: 978-1-78099-615-8

ebook: 978-1-78099-616-5

Traditional Witchcraft for the Woods and Forests

A Witch's Guide to the Woodland with Guided Meditations and Pathworking

Melusine Draco

A Witch's guide to walking alone in the woods, with guided meditations and pathworking.

Paperback: 978-1-84694-803-9

ebook: 978-1-84694-804-6

Wild Earth, Wild Soul
A Manual for an Ecstatic Culture
Bill Pfeiffer
Imagine a nature-based culture so alive and so connected,
spreading like wildfire. This book is the first flame...
Paperback: 978-1-78099-187-0
ebook: 978-1-78099-188-7

Naming the Goddess
Trevor Greenfield
Naming the Goddess is written by more than 80 adherents and
scholars of the Goddess and Goddess Spirituality.
Paperback: 978-1-78279-476-9
ebook: 978-1-78279-475-2

Shapeshifting into Higher Consciousness
Heal and Transform Yourself and our World with Ancient and
Modern Shamanic Methods
Llyn Roberts
Ancient and modern methods that you can use every day
to transform yourself and make a positive difference in the
world.
Paperback: 978-1-84694-843-5
ebook: 978-1-84694-844-2

Find more titles and sign up to our readers' newsletter at
http://www.johnhuntpublishing.com/paganism.
Follow us on Facebook at
https://www.facebook.com/MoonBooks and Twitter at
https://twitter.com/MoonBooksJHP. Most titles are
published in paperback and as an ebook. Paperbacks are
available in physical bookshops. Both print and ebook
editions are available online. Readers of ebooks can click
on the live links in the titles to order.